Three Ir

PAULA MEEHAN was born in Dublin. She studied at Trinity College, Dublin and Eastern Washington University. She has written plays and collaborated extensively with visual artists, film-makers and musicians, and is involved in arts projects with prisoners and community groups.

MARY O'MALLEY was born in Connemara and educated at University College, Galway. She has taught writing in prisons, schools and universities, and worked extensively with musicians. In addition to publishing five volumes of poetry, she has edited two books of children's writing.

EAVAN BOLAND was born in Dublin and studied in Ireland, London and New York. In 1994 she was poet-in-residence at the National Maternity Hospital in Dublin. She has received numerous awards for her writing. She teaches at Stanford University where she is director of the Creative Writing Program.

Also by Paula Meehan from Carcanet

Dharmakaya

Also by Mary O'Malley from Carcanet

The Boning Hall

Also by Eavan Boland from Carcanet

Poetry
Code
Collected Poems
In a Time of Violence
The Lost Land
Night Feed
Outside History
Selected Poems

Prose
Object Lessons

PAULA MEEHAN, MARY O'MALLEY,
EAVAN BOLAND

Three Irish Poets
An Anthology

Edited by Eavan Boland

CARCANET

Acknowledgements

'Lullaby', The Pattern', 'Child Burial', 'The Dark Twin', 'Well' by Paula Meehan, included by kind permission of the author and The Gallery Press, Loughcrew, Oldcastle, County Meath, Ireland. From *The Man Who Was Marked by Winter* (1991). 'My Father Perceived as a Vision of St Francis', 'City', 'Would you jump into my grave as quick?', 'Folktale', 'Blessing', 'Home' by Paula Meehan, included by kind permission of the author and The Gallery Press, Loughcrew, Oldcastle, County Meath, Ireland. From *Pillow Talk* (1994).

Poems by Mary O'Malley first published in *A Consideration of Silk* (Salmon Publishing, 1990), *Where the Rocks Float* (Salmon Publishing, 1993), *The Knife in the Wave* (Salmon Publishing, 1997) and *Asylum Road* (Salmon Publishing, 2001) included in this collection by kind permission of the author and Salmon Publishing, Knockeven, Cliffs of Moher, County Clare, Ireland.

Poems by Eavan Boland included in this selection were first published in *New Territory* (Allen Figgis Press, 1967), *Night Feed* (Arlen House/Carcanet, 1982), *The Journey* (Arlen House/Carcanet 1986), *Outside History* (Carcanet/W.W. Norton, 1990), *In a Time of Violence* (Carcanet/W.W. Norton, 1994), *The Lost Land* (Carcanet/W.W. Norton, 1998), *Code* (Carcanet/W.W. Norton, 2001).

First published in Great Britain in 2003 by
Carcanet Press Limited
Alliance House
Cross Street
Manchester M2 7AQ

Individual authors' selections and introductions copyright individual author © 2003

Editor's introduction copyright Eavan Boland © 2003

The right of Eavan Boland to be recognised as the editor of this book has been asserted by her in accordance with the Copyright, Designs and Patents Act of 1988

A CIP catalogue record for this book is available from the British Library

ISBN 1 85754 683 0

The publisher acknowledges financial assistance from Arts Council England

Typeset in Monotype Garamond by XL Publishing Services, Tiverton

CONTENTS

Mary O'Malley

Eavan Boland

INTRODUCTION

I

There is a painting in the room I work in. It hangs on a wall opposite my desk. There is no way of avoiding it. It establishes a frank, eyeline contact whenever I look up. It has been there for years: I want it to be there. What's more, its history is so particular and revealing that I have included it here as a way of framing these poems.

It is a watercolour of a field. An almost surreal field at that. Although it appears to be harvest time, the earth is a mulberry-grey and the sky just a few smoky daubs. A woman in a burnt-red skirt is bending over the ground. There are cottages, a horse and a blue scribble for the hills.

All of this was done by my mother in the 1940s. She was then competing for a commission to paint a mural on the wall of the Bakers' Union in Dublin. The entry required twelve large watercolour sketches to suggest the finished wall panels. Every one of them had to be – directly or indirectly – on the theme of bread. This was the twelfth.

The field is seen through an open window. It is intended as an image of Ireland. And Ireland, moreover, at this high moment of survival: a nation celebrated as a small harmony of blues and unlikely blends of greys and pinks and ochres. A country made into an emblem of need and nourishment.

Two writers are looking out, one standing and one sitting. The man at the desk, with his unkempt hair and dark coat, is almost certainly a poet. The other man stands at his shoulder. They are watching the woman and the blue hills. There is nothing naturalistic about any of it. The distances are odd and the men's faces are blank. Nevertheless, the images make the argument: the woman is laying seed and making the harvest. The men are shaping the language which will define her meaning as well as their own. The syllogism is near to hand: men nourish a country with individual acts of art and language. Women can only feed it with the daily and ordinary work of their hands: with the communal task

My mother won the commission. The murals were painted. The image of the woman seed-layer and the male poet were inscribed on the walls of the Bakers' Union. Time moved on. Progress arrived. The building was destroyed to make way for new developments. The mulberry harvest field ended up in the dust of a builder's yard.

I keep the painting in sight both as witness and warning. There is a quick, lyric confidence about it which I admire. A grace. A rapid traffic between the real and the mythic. But there is something painful in it for me as well. The painter was a woman. The artists in the painting are men. Does it matter? I think it does.

'For most of history, Anonymous was a woman', writes Virginia Woolf. As a young Irish painter of her time my mother could imagine the nation. She could imagine the nation's art. And yet she could not imagine herself as a woman and a maker at the centre of her own statement: enacting, shaping, defining it. There is no discredit to my mother in this. In so many ways she was exemplary. Besides, imagination can be mired in the shackles and permissions of its time. But there is a harsh truth here nonetheless. My mother could take an Irish field and make it a beautiful, mulberry site of action. She could suggest the private connections for the public art. But when the image of the maker was made she was absent. In a poignant and crucial way, her imagination failed her at the moment she needed it most.

II

We need imagination. Not just for the actions commonly associated with it, of reading and writing. We also need it for its less obvious powers – to shift and re-settle the fixed counters of expectation and assumption. It has taken a long time for women poets to place themselves at the centre of the Irish poem. It has been an arduous journey from object to author. It has required difficult engagements with political and cultural realities for them to stand at that window. And see themselves standing there.

'If I must not, because of my sex, have this freedom', wrote Aphra Behn, 'I lay down my quill, and you shall hear no more of me.' Now however, more and more is heard from Irish women poets. The work of Nuala ni Dhomnaill, Eilean ni Chuilleanain, Medbh McGuckian, Rita Ann Higgins, Moya Cannon, Vona Groarke, Sinead Morrissey – to mention only a few names – shows the power of this emergence. They are not included here, only because this is a grouping of Carcanet poets. But my references to the complex and far-reaching effects of this poetry also imply the presence and distinction of their work.

Women poets in Ireland offer a new narrative of place and perception. 'We are citizens of an age as well as a State', said Schiller and both have changed at a rapid pace in recent years. For that very reason, it may seem hard to calibrate the exact difference a woman poet makes to the writing of a poem. Nevertheless, it stands to reason that the entrance into the Irish poem of a constituency which was once silent – both in the society beyond the poem and in the poem itself – has the power to alter fixed boundaries. Poems are being written now in which both the subject and the stance are radically different from what went before. Above all, those demarcations between the local and national and domestic, which once seemed such a given in Irish poetry, have become luminously unsettled in poems by women.

III

The work of three poets is presented here. Paula Meehan, Mary O'Malley and myself belong to different Irish generations. Each group of poems here has been selected by the individual poet. There always seems to me a particular value – a sort of invisible writing – in the way poets select their own poems. That hidden shape, that small trajectory of purpose and meaning a poet holds in her own head about her own work, is therefore an integral part of what's offered here.

The work is arranged chronologically and it is possible at times to see a new Ireland creeping to the edges of the poems and then slipping inside with a word, a phrase, a reference. When I began to write and publish there were no computers in Ireland, no cable television, no nightclubs along Leeson Street. The emigrant boat still existed. The streets emptied out on the weekend. Traffic was navigable. The transatlantic phone was a luxury. The Ireland of prosperity and modern communications was not yet on the horizon.

Therefore it is a particular and informative strength that Paula Meehan and Mary O'Malley, both leading poets of their generation, are also superb poets of place. Their places, of course, are widely separated. Paula Meehan comes from Dublin, from the inner city. Mary O'Malley was born in Connemara. The distances between a city so deeply implicated in the narrative of conquest and resistance as Dublin, and the beautiful, harsh landscape of the western seaboard may seem almost infinite. And certainly the lexicon of iron, water and quick-witted reflection is bracingly different from the elegies and elements of the west.

But there is common ground as well: a shared strength. Above all, there are poems by both poets which reveal the local in an entirely new light: as a charged, intimate space in the Irish poem. In lines, cadences, whole poems it becomes the brokerage between the national and the domestic, between the public space and the hidden life.

An example is Paula Meehan's 'The Pattern'. This seems to me a poem which re-defines the Irish poem in a compelling way. To start with, this is not a conventional landscape. The figures are awry. There is something skewed, off-balance about it all. A daughter looks back at her mother's life through a lens of grief and language. What is remarkable is how the private and secret life of a woman is balanced in the poem with the public interrogations of the speaker. The mother's is a hidden, afflicted world. The poem does not try to drag it to the light. But the technical ease with which the speaker of the poem moves from private grief to public reference sets the tone:

> *Little has come down to me of hers,*
> *a sewing machine, a wedding band,*
> *a clutch of photos, the sting of her hand*
> *across my face*

What is compelling here is the harsh inventory of inheritance – but not just that. Also the way that the background and foreground of the Irish poem – so often full of conventional perspective – are collapsed so that the location is discoverable in the person, and not the other way around. The city is hardly mentioned and yet the Dublin of harsh colours and hard lives is made powerfully available:

> *First she'd scrub the floor with Sunlight soap,*
> *an armreach at a time. When her knees grew sore*
> *she'd break for a cup of tea, then start again*
> *at the door with lavender polish. The smell*
> *would percolate back through the flat to us,*
> *her brood banished to the bedroom.*

> *And as she buffed the wax to a high shine*
> *did she catch her own face coming clear?*
> *Did she net a glimmer of her true self?*
> *Did her mirror tell her what mine tells me?*

'The Pattern' opens a new space. Into it comes that heartbreaking light of real lives – of women and their daughters caught in the strange and contradictory zone of colony. Unconsoling and anti-pastoral, it offers a fresh and disturbing commentary on place – that frequent generic of the Irish poem: place is no longer the site of history or the source of elegy. It is that edgy in-between terrain easing out from under the struggle between silence and expression. It is what is left rather than what is there:

> *I was sizing*
> *up the world beyond our flat patch by patch*

daily after school, and fitting each surprising
city street to city square to diamond. I'd watch

the Liffey for hours pulsing to the sea
and the coming and going of ships,
certain that one day it would carry me
to Zanzibar, Bombay, the land of the Ethiops.

IV

'No man', wrote Patrick Kavanagh of his townland, 'ever loved that landscape and even some of the people more than I.' Irish poetry has taken its shapes and influences from far and wide. As a young poet, I found Kavanagh one of the most enabling predecessors. When he left Monaghan and came to Dublin at the end of the 1930s he was a young, dissident poet. In leaving the silences of his own place to come to the self-conscious and literary city he was enacting the classical pastoral trajectory: leaving the real to be tempted by the ideal.

His sweet-natured and anti-authoritarian spirit resisted the temptation. Had he not – according to pastoral convention – he might have watched his own powerful feeling for place elaborated into the magic and shelter of an ideal relation. He could have been screen-tested for a minor place in the Irish Revival. And certainly, in the most declamatory of its writings, the Revival was shaping and re-shaping Ireland into a pastoral entity – a place sanitised of its defeats, silences and shames. Kavanagh would have none of it. 'When I came to Dublin', he had written, 'the Irish Literary Affair was still booming. It was the notion that Dublin was a literary metropolis and Ireland as invented and patented by Yeats, Lady Gregory and Synge, a spiritual entity.'

There is an allegory here: a suppressed narrative of the challenges and obstacles faced by Irish women poets. In writing out of their lives and experiences, women poets of my generation were doing what all poets do. But they were doing it in the context of an Irish poem which for more than a hundred years had assigned the poet and the subject a fixed place to speak from and be spoken of. The Irish poem, even at its best, was a bardic and high enterprise. Women poets gradually came to their strengths: they could write of a charged and disowned life which, in and of itself, linked them to the silences and secrets of Irish history. They were in painful possession a devalued subject matter. This in itself was enough to shift and re-order the fixities of the poem they inherited.

Hence the importance of Kavanagh's resistance. He showed the value of a perspective that skews those already in place. The way in which a poem or a tradition is changed is elusive. But Kavanagh's anger – expressed in many of his prose writings – at the idea of the traffic between a much loved locale and a literary centre which would only agree to legitimise it on certain terms, is still instructive.

It is also – this negotiation between inheritance and instinct – a rich theme in some of the poems here. It is present in Mary O'Malley's poem 'The Shape of Saying', which provides at first a witty and oblique view: almost a micro-satire of a troubled linguistic tradition:

> *They call it Received English*
> *as if it was a gift you got*
> *by dint of primogeniture.*
> *Maybe it was. Old gold words*
> *toned like concert violins,*
> *tuned to talk to God.*

But the poem turns dark and poignant. It surprises and catches the reader. The idea of how a language – for that read a tradition or a canon – can be shaped and re-shaped, can be shocked into reality, comes with a rare eloquence:

> *It was hard and slippery as pebbles*
> *full of cornered consonants*
> *and pinched vowels, all said*
> *from the front of the mouth*
> *no softness, no sorrow, no sweet lullabies*
> *until we took it by the neck and shook it.*
>
> *We sheared it, carded it, fleeced it*
> *and finally wove it*
> *into something of our own,*
> *fit for curses and blessings*

V

Between 1900 and 1950 Irish poetry was tempered by far-reaching change. A new nation. A lexicon of new freedoms. An urgent need for self-expression. These circumstances were a forcing-house of powerful, illuminating lyrics. 'Art is a reality, not a definition', wrote Benjamin Haydon. Under these pressures, literature in Ireland re-defined itself. The excitement of those years and those exigencies pushed Irish poetry in new directions. Yeats, Kavanagh, MacNeice,

Devlin – all, in various ways and with various success, responded to the challenge.

Yet, with few exceptions, women were not part of this. One of the reasons may be that their relation to the new nation was as complex and shadowed as to the literary tradition. The apparent end of colony in Ireland left women with new laws, new strictures – and the unspoken assumptions which go with those – and new silences.

The effects of this exclusion were significant both for the society and its poetry. Many fine poems were written; many changes were reflected in them. But the lack of the voice and vision of women left certain elements of Irish poetry unchallenged. For instance, the old association between the public and political remained in place. It was a nineteenth-century inscription – something written deep in the Irish poem.

The reverse is true also. The emergence of women has made a new space in the Irish poem. The dailyness, detail and ordinariness of a woman's life in contemporary Ireland – the very source of suspicion in some cases – has become a powerful lens on the life of the republic. In the work of women poets, again and again, the so-called domestic, with its insistence on the revealed private life, shifts the political poem into a private realm where its priorities are re-examined. Nothing is lost by this. The old registers of power and rhetoric are still there. But a whole new vocabulary of sense and impression has been admitted. This is the place where women's poetry comes to the centre of Irish poetry: where it re-writes and reclaims and adds immeasurably to the rich store of the past.

Two poems in this book provide striking examples of this. The first, by Paula Meehan, is called 'My Father Perceived As a Vision of St Francis'. The scene is unassuming, delicately drawn. An early morning in a Dublin suburb. Frost on the roof-slates. A father, seen by his daughter as older and more frail than she had quite realised, unlatching the back door and going into the garden. When the birds come from other neighbourhoods, flying in for the crumbs he will throw, we know at one level that this is an entirely private and local moment. But at another level a wonderful series of inferences has been started and continues: of faith, of the iconography of Catholicism, of shifts of power between a daughter and a father, of the ordinary landscape of a suburb claimed as a visionary moment:

> *They came then: birds*
> *of every size, shape, colour; they came*
> *from the hedges and shrubs,*
> *from eaves and garden sheds,*

from the industrial estate, outlying fields,
from Dubber Cross they came
and the ditches of the North Road.
The garden was a pandemonium

when my father threw up his hands
and tossed the crumbs to the air. The sun

cleared O'Reilly's chimney
and he was suddenly radiant,
a perfect vision of St Francis,
    made whole, made young again,
    in a Finglas garden.

Similarly, in Mary O'Malley's poem 'Tracing' the deep conflicts between art, expression, exclusion are put in the context of the customary lives of the Irish west coast. At the start of the poem, a woman looks at two men speaking. One is a poet, the other a fisherman. Where does she fit in? This question – awkward, painful and necessary – drives the poem:

They sit under a western window
a poet and a fisherman
tracing the genealogy of pucans. Back
to the summer of nineteen-twenty-seven,
back to a rotting template in the sand.
Between them they could raise the dead.

And I forever outside looking in
am thinking of women measuring
the rising skirts of the wind, scanning
the swollen sea for one speck
to lift out of a trough,
a miracle of engine or sail

when I would rather be there
beside the black-haired men,
appeasing God with the swift sacrifice
of net to knife. What keeps me out,
the uncontented daughter?

VI

What keeps me out? That question echoed through my youth. When I was beginning as a poet in Ireland there seemed to be barriers and resistances that were hard to define and yet had the unwelcome power to define me. I found that women's poetry might be considered worthwhile as just that: but its entitlement to be at the centre of Irish poetry – to shape the present and re-shape the past – was contested. That such an exclusion was a deep ethical contradiction in a post-colonial literature did not seem to occur to many people – or at least not enough of them to stop me being puzzled and concerned. At the time, it seemed burdensome to me to have to try to analyse this as well as write poems. Later I changed my mind. I came to believe that definitions were necessary. That they would help to clear out that mysterious space of shadows around the poem I was writing.

Years ago I came to realise that the reasons for the initial resistance were the very ones that make women's writing so essential in Ireland. In a country whose past is so shaped by oppression it is the sites outside history which matter most. Above all, countries injured by colony are particularly troubled in their relation to powerlessness. Women's experience had little place in the heroic interpretation of Irish history – a version which has had more influence on Irish literature than is often admitted.

This book shows that the shadows are less. And certain poems here – like so many others by contemporary Irish women – have been instrumental in the lessening of those shadows. The language of lived experience, of daily encounter, of the ordinary world, has proved to be a source and not a stumbling block for vision. Paula Meehan's Dublin streets, alive with incident and memory, as well as the thwarted love and confident visions in her poems, create both a new sound and reveal an old silence The same is true of Mary O'Malley's Connemara with its echoes of lost languages and new energies. But the images of a changing Ireland are only a fraction of the story.

'When the soul of a man is born in this country there are nets flung at it to hold it back from flight.' Stephen Dedalus's exasperated comment, with a shift of gender, is especially applicable. Irish society was suspicious of the possible association between the concepts of woman and poet – between a category so broadly and indulgently defined and one so narrowly and tensely construed. In a certain sense, societies are right to be wary of these associations: once the tensions and expansions of a new language enter a literature there is no going back.

The association between the woman and the poet – the successful blending of those identities in my generation – has certainly changed Irish poetry. But there is more to it than that. It has also radically altered the idea of the Irish poet. If a poet can be not just the voice of a history but the witness to a silence, then the Irish poem stands to gain immeasurably from that authority. Many of the poems here are traceable to a lost Irish past which might once have seemed irrecoverable. But the poems here recover it. There are many stanzas, lines, lyrics here where women, unlike in my mother's painting, stand at the window: where the maker and the made poem are visible together. Inscribing new voices in a tradition can be disruptive. Nevertheless women's voices are now deeply marked on Irish poetry. I cannot believe that anyone who loves Irish literature, and its long struggle towards the light, would wish it otherwise.

Eavan Boland
Dundrum 2002

PAULA MEEHAN

PAULA MEEHAN

Paula Meehan was born in Dublin in 1955, the eldest of a family of six. She grew up in the north inner city where she attended the Central Model Schools. Later the family moved to Finglas, to a council estate north of the city where she began her secondary education with the Holy Faith Sisters. Expelled from that school, she completed her intermediary education on her own. As a teenager she was writing song lyrics for local Finglas bands and published her first poems in magazines put together with other kids. She studied for her Leaving Certificate in Whitehall House Senior Girls' School, and at seventeen she entered Trinity College, Dublin where she completed a Bachelor of Arts degree in English, History and Classical Civilisation. As a student she supported herself with work in bars and restaurants and as a member of a street theatre troupe, The Childrens' T Company. After university she wandered through Europe, living for a while in both Germany and Crete. From 1981 to 1983 she studied at Eastern Washington University where she received a Master of Fine Arts degree. After her studies she travelled throughout the north west along the Columbia River, working as a fruit harvester, eventually arriving in San Francisco.

Her first two collections of poetry , *Return and No Blame* and *Reading the Sky* were from a small Dublin publisher, now defunct, Beaver Row Press. They came out in the mid-1980s in small editions, hand set by Kevin Byrne, printed on an old platen press. The Gallery Press published the two collections which brought her work to the notice of a wider audience, *The Man Who Was Marked by Winter* and *Pillow Talk*, in the 1990s.

She has written plays for both adults and children, collaborated with visual artists, written poems to accompany film works, has had poems choreographed to specially composed scores for contemporary dance companies, and had poems set to music by artists as diverse as the avant garde composer John Wolf Brennan and the folk singer Christy Moore.

As a teacher and moderater of poetry workshops Paula Meehan has held residencies in many universities, including Trinity College, Dublin, where she was Writing Fellow in Residence twenty years after she was a student there. She ran the National Writers' Workshop out of University College, Galway and has been Writer by Association at

University College, Dublin. She spent many years running workshops in the prisons of the Republic, mostly with women prisoners, though she has also worked in the high security Arbour Hill male prison and with the political prisoners in Portlaoise before the amnesty negotiated as part of the peace process. She has worked with community groups throughout Ireland and has a continuing engagement with education and arts projects in the community where she spent her childhood – the north inner city.

Paula Meehan has received many awards for her work, including Arts Council Bursaries, the Butler Award for Poetry of the Irish American Cultural Institute, and the Marten Toonder Award for Literature; her most recent collection of poems *Dharmakaya* (from Carcanet Press) received the Denis Devlin Memorial Award from the Irish Arts Council. She was elected a member of Aosdána in 1996.

Lullaby

for Brenda Meehan

My sister is sleeping
and makes small murmurs
as she turns in a dream

she is swinging a child
under the shade of
a lilac tree blooming

in a garden in springtime
my sister is sleeping.

The rain falls
on Finglas
to each black roof

it lashes a story
of time on the ocean
of moon on the river

and flashes down drainpipes
into deep gutters.

My sister is sleeping
her hands full of blossoms
plucked for the child

who dreams in her womb
rocked in tall branches
close to the stars

where my sister is sleeping
within her small child.

The Pattern

Little has come down to me of hers,
a sewing machine, a wedding band,
a clutch of photos, the sting of her hand
across my face in one of our wars

when we had grown bitter and apart.
Some say that's the fate of the eldest daughter.
I wish now she'd lasted till after
I'd grown up. We might have made a new start

as women without tags like *mother*, *wife*,
sister, *daughter*, taken our chances from there.
At forty-two she headed for god knows where.
I've never gone back to visit her grave.

*

First she'd scrub the floor with Sunlight soap,
an armreach at a time. When her knees grew sore
she'd break for a cup of tea, then start again
at the door with lavender polish. The smell
would percolate back through the flat to us,
her brood banished to the bedroom.

And as she buffed the wax to a high shine
did she catch her own face coming clear?
Did she net a glimmer of her true self?
Did her mirror tell her what mine tells me?

I have her shrug and go on
knowing history has brought her to her knees.

She'd call us in and let us skate around
in our socks. We'd grow solemn as planets
in an intricate orbit about her.

*

She's bending over crimson cloth,
the younger kids are long in bed.
Late summer. Cold enough for a fire,
she works by fading light
to remake an old dress for me.
It's first day back at school tomorrow.

*

'Pure lambswool. Plenty of wear in it yet.
You know I wore this when I went out with your Da.
I was supposed to be down in a friend's house,
your Granda caught us at the corner.
He dragged me in by the hair – it was long as yours then –
in front of the whole street.
He called your Da every name under the sun,
cornerboy, lout; I needn't tell you
what he called me. He shoved my whole head
under the kitchen tap, took a scrubbing brush
and carbolic soap and in ice-cold water he scrubbed
every speck of lipstick and mascara off my face.
Christ but he was a right tyrant, your Granda.
It'll be over my dead body that anyone harms a hair of your head.'

*

She must have stayed up half the night
to finish the dress. I found it airing at the fire,
three new copybooks on the table and a bright
bronze nib, St Christopher strung on a silver wire,

as if I were embarking on a perilous journey
to uncharted realms. I wore that dress
with little grace. To me it spelt poverty,
the stigma of the second hand. I grew enough to pass

it on by Christmas to the next in line. I was sizing
up the world beyond our flat patch by patch
daily after school, and fitting each surprising
city street to city square to diamond. I'd watch

the Liffey for hours pulsing to the sea
and the coming and going of ships,
certain that one day it would carry me
to Zanzibar, Bombay, the land of the Ethiops.

*

There's a photo of her taken in the Phoenix Park
alone on a bench surrounded by roses
as if she had been born to formal gardens.
She stares out as if unaware
that any human hand held the camera, wrapped
entirely in her own shadow, the world beyond her
already a dream, already lost. She's
eight months pregnant. Her last child.

*

Her steel needles sparked and clacked,
the only other sound a settling coal
or her sporadic mutter
at a hard part in the pattern.
She favoured sensible shades:
Moss Green, Mustard, Beige.

I dreamt a robe of a colour
so pure it became a word.

Sometimes I'd have to kneel
an hour before her by the fire,
a skein around my outstretched hands,
while she rolled wool into balls.
If I swam like a kite too high
amongst the shadows on the ceiling
or flew like a fish in the pools
of pulsing light, she'd reel me firmly
home, she'd land me at her knees.

Tongues of flame in her dark eyes,
she'd say, 'One of these days I must
teach you to follow a pattern.'

Child Burial

Your coffin looked unreal,
fancy as a wedding cake.

I chose your grave clothes with care,
your favourite stripey shirt,

your blue cotton trousers.
They smelt of woodsmoke, of October,

your own smell there too.
I chose a gansy of handspun wool,

warm and fleecy for you. It is
so cold down in the dark.

No light can reach you and teach you
the paths of wild birds,

the names of the flowers,
the fishes, the creatures.

Ignorant you must remain
of the sun and its work,

my lamb, my calf, my eaglet,
my cub, my kid, my nestling,

my suckling, my colt. I would spin
time back, take you again

within my womb, your amniotic lair,
and further spin you back

through nine waxing months
to the split seeding moment

you chose to be made flesh,
word within me.

I'd cancel the love feast
the hot night of your making.

I would travel alone
to a quiet mossy place,

you would spill from me into the earth
drop by bright red drop.

The Dark Twin

You believe
they contract when you turn to the window –
there's a girl in pink passing
you might or might not know
down a street you say history will be made on
as the woman you hold turns to your eyes.
Anemones, she tells you, make the same sound as pupils.
Pishew, pishew, were you close enough
in rockpool silence, is what you would hear.

And you believe
she'll turn again and again to your eyes
as you hold her. Show your stored wisdom
in a ritual of healing. Your hands move
over her dark form. She can't refuse you.
Gulls cross the sky, bells sound for first Mass.
You know she'll seek you for she is
your dark twin. Her eyes don't reflect you.
Her pupils are still as the dark pool
she grew from. She names you *diablo.*
If you enter her now you can teach her
the nature of history, the city that's made her.
She'll name a price later and say you've had
her cheaply. She'll be just. You won't haggle
but find the exact change and count it into her palm.

And you believe
she'll return and desire you once more –
more than her own life, more than her darkness.
This you know surely as you glance over
her eyes to the girl in pink passing.
You move above her: by your ritual rocking
you'll move her to tears.
She'll learn to accept love though still
you must pay her the exact amount due.

And you believe
you can quieten her sobs in the morning
when she tells you again
how the world will succumb to men in dark uniforms.
You believe she has stood, her face to a stone wall,
while the men cock their rifles and wait for the order.
You know she's been there. You know you can heal her.
The burns from the bombings will ease as you rock her.
The legs that are mangled made whole for fast dancing.
Her sobs will be songs for the rearing of children.
Still you must pay her the exact amount due.

And you believe all this
as you turn from the window,
the girl in pink passing at the moment
you enter your dark twin. Your pupils
dilate, your breath as it leaves you
makes the one word you can never repay her.

Well

I know this path by magic not by sight.
Behind me on the hillside the cottage light
is like a star that's gone astray. The moon
is waning fast, each blade of grass a rune
inscribed by hoarfrost. This path's well worn.
I lug a bucket by bramble and blossoming blackthorn.
I know this path by magic not by sight.
Next morning when I come home quite unkempt
I cannot tell what happened at the well.
You spurn my explanation of a sex spell
cast by the spirit that guards the source
that boils deep in the belly of the earth,
even when I show you what lies strewn
in my bucket – a golden waning moon,
seven silver stars, our own porch light,
your face at the window staring into the dark.

My Father Perceived as a Vision of St Francis

for Brendan Kennelly

It was the piebald horse in next door's garden
frightened me out of a dream
with her dawn whinny. I was back
in the boxroom of the house,
my brother's room now,
full of ties and sweaters and secrets.
Bottles chinked on the doorstep,
the first bus pulled up to the stop.
The rest of the house slept

except for my father. I heard
him rake the ash from the grate,
plug in the kettle, hum a snatch of a tune.
Then he unlocked the back door
and stepped out into the garden.

Autumn was nearly done, the first frost
whitened the slates of the estate.
He was older than I had reckoned,
his hair completely silver,
and for the first time I saw the stoop
of his shoulder, saw that
his leg was stiff. What's he at?
So early and still stars in the west?

They came then: birds
of every size, shape, colour; they came
from the hedges and shrubs,
from eaves and garden sheds,
from the industrial estate, outlying fields,
from Dubber Cross they came
and the ditches of the North Road.
The garden was a pandemonium
when my father threw up his hands
and tossed the crumbs to the air. The sun

cleared O'Reilly's chimney
and he was suddenly radiant,
a perfect vision of St Francis,
made whole, made young again,
in a Finglas garden.

City

Hearth

What is the fire you draw to
when you clutch each other
between the sheets? What cold do
you fear? What drives you near
madness, the jealousy you daily
bear? That tyrant time
sifting through the glass. Tell me
a story, not in rhyme
or made up fancy but plain
as the ash in the grate.
The window pane rattles, the rain
beats about the house. Late
drinkers are turfed from the bar. Wind
snatches their song, tosses it down-
river to the sea pulsing in your mind.
You slip your moorings, cruise the town.

Night Walk

Out here you can breathe.
Between showers, the street
empty. Forget your lover
faithless in the chilly bed
who'll wake soon and wonder
if you've left for good.
Granite under your feet
glitters, nearby a siren. Threat

or a promise? You take Fumbally Lane
to the Blackpitts, cut back by the canal.
Hardly a sound you've made, creature
of night in grey jeans and desert boots,
familiar of shade.
                    Listen. The train
bearing chemicals to Mayo, a dog far off, the fall
of petals to the paths of the Square,
a child screaming in a third floor flat.

On Mount Street high heels clack,
stumble in their rhythm, resume.
Let her too get home safe, your prayer,
not like that poor woman last night
dragged down Glovers Alley, raped there,
battered to a pulp. Still unnamed.
Your key in the door, you've made it back,
a chorus of birds predicting light.

Man Sleeping

How deep are you, how far under?
Here's rosemary I stole on my walk
and the first lilac from the Square.
I lay them on the quilt. You talk
in your dreaming. *I am the beating tide,*
mine is the shore. Taste of the sea,
pulse of my heart. *Don't leave me,*
don't leave me. I dive beneath
and you stiffen to my mouth.
You'll be deep within me when you wake,
your pulse my own. Wave that I ride,
I'll take everything before you break.

Full Moon

She's up there. You'd know the pull,
stretching you tight as a drumhead,
anywhere. This morning lull
between the alarm and quitting the bed
you consider the scrawb on his back –
sigil of grief: the thumbscrew, the rack.
A paleskin staked on the desert floor
bound at ankle, at neck, at wrist,
no cavalry in sight to even the score.
This is the knife in the gut; this is its twist.

She's up there. Tonight they'll dish out
more downers in prison, in the mental
asylum, tonight there'll be more blood spilt
on the street, and you will howl
to her through the tattered cloud scrawled
across the windowpane, a howl fated
by the blemish on his shoulderblade.
Ask yourself: *to what shapechanger has he mated?*

On the Warpath

The full moon is drawing you tight
as a drumhead. Your face in the mirror
is cloudy, overcast. No sunny spells;
frost inland tonight.

Reconnoitre the terrain of the heart,
scan for high ground. Ambush, skirmish,
reprisal, this deadly game you play.
Give as good as you get.

Choose protective colouring, camouflage,
know your foe, every move of him,
every bar of his battle hymn.
Though the outward face is dead cas-

ual, within the self is coiled:
unsprung, the human, suddenly, wild.

Would you jump into my grave as quick?

Would you jump into my grave as quick?
my granny would ask when one of us took
her chair by the fire. You, woman,
done up to the nines, red lips a come on,
your breath reeking of drink
and your black eye on my man tonight
in a Dublin bar, think
first of the steep drop, the six dark feet.

Folktale

A young man falls in love with Truth and searches the wide world for her. He finds her in a small house, in a clearing, in a forest. She is old and stooped. He swears himself to her service – to chop wood, to carry water, to collect the root, the stem, the leaf, the flowering top, the seed of each plant she needs for her work.

Years go by. One day the young man wakes up longing for a child. He goes to the old woman and asks to be released from his oath so that he may return to the world. *Certainly*, she says, *but on one condition: you must tell them that I am young and that I am beautiful.*

Blessing

for Tony Curtis

Not to the colony for artists
not to the walled university
but to the demented asylum
I'll go when the moon is up
in the day sky, I'll go

and snatch a song from a stranger's mouth.

They have been speaking so long
in riddles, they teach you
the heart for a child breaking,
the heart breaking for a child
is nothing more than a shift
of light on a slate roof
after rain, and the elderberry's
purpling shade is as much
as you'll know of grieving.

They have been speaking so long
in riddles the world believes at last
in enigma, the earth understands
her beguiling work –
      leaf, stone, wave.

To the demented asylum I'll go
for succour from a stranger's mouth:
      leaf crown you
            wave repeat you
                  stone secure your grave

Home

I am the blind woman finding her way home by a map of tune.
When the song that is in me is the song I hear from the world
I'll be home. It's not written down and I don't remember the words.
I know when I hear it I'll have made it myself. I'll be home.

A version I heard once in Leitrim was close, a wet Tuesday night
in the Sean Relig bar. I had come for the session, I stayed
for the vision and lore. The landlord called time,
the music dried up, the grace notes were pitched to the dark.
When the jukebox blared out *I'd only four senses and he left me senseless,*
I'd no choice but to take to the road. On Grafton Street in
                                   November
I heard a mighty sound: a travelling man with a didgeridoo
blew me clear to Botany Bay. The tune too far back to live in
but scribed on my bones. In a past life I may have been Kangaroo,
rocked in my dreamtime, convict ships coming o'er the foam.

In the Puzzle Factory one winter I was sure I was home.
The talking in tongues, the riddles, the rhymes, struck a chord
that cut through the pharmaceutical haze. My rhythm catatonic,
I lulled myself back to the womb, my mother's heart
beating the drum of herself and her world. I was tricked
by her undersong, just close enough to my own. I took then
to dancing; I spun like a Dervish. I swear I heard the subtle
music of the spheres. It's no place to live – but,

out there in space, on your own hung aloft the night.
The tune was in truth a mechanical drone;
I was a pitiful monkey jigging on cue. I came back to earth
with a land, to rain on my face, to sun in my hair. And grateful too.

The wisewomen say you must live in your skin, call *it* home,
no matter how battered or broken, misused by the world, you can
heal.
This morning a letter arrived on the nine o'clock post.
The Department of Historical Reparation and who did I blame?
The Nuns? Your Mother? The State? *Tick box provided,*
we'll consider your case. I'm burning my soapbox, I'm taking
the very next train. A citizen of nowhere, nothing to my name.
I'm on my last journey. Though my lines are all wonky
they spell me a map that makes sense. Where the song that is in me
is the song I hear from the world, I'll set down my burdens
and sleep. The spot that I lie on at last the place I'll call home.

Dharmakaya

for Thom McGinty

When you step out into death
with a deep breath,
the last you'll ever take
in this shape,

remember the first step on the street –
the footfall and the shadow
of its fall – into silence. Breathe
slow-

ly out before the foot finds solid earth again,
before the city rain
has washed all trace
of your step away.

Remember a time in the woods, a path
you walked so gently
no twig snapped
no bird startled.

Between breath and no breath
your hands cupped your own death,
a gift, a bowl of grace
you brought home to us –

become a still pool
in the anarchic flow, the street's
unceasing carnival
of haunted and redeemed.

The View from Under the Table

was the best view and the table itself kept the sky
from falling. The world was fringed with red velvet tassels;
whatever play ran in that room the tablecloth was curtains for.
I was the audience. Listen to me laughing. Listen
to me weeping. I was a child. What did I know?

Except that the moon was a porcelain globe and swung from a
                                        brass chain. O
that wasn't the moon at all. The moon was my true love. Oak was
                                        my roof and
under the table no one could see you. My granny could see me.
Out, she'd say. Out. And up on her lap the smell of kitchen and
                                        sleep.
She'd rock me. She'd lull me. No one was kinder.

What ails you child? I never told her. Not
one word would cross my lips. Shadows I'd say. I don't like the
                                        shadows.
They're waiting to snatch me. There at the turn of the stairs.
On the landing. To the right of the wardrobe. In the fridge, white
                                        ghosts.
Black ghosts in the coal shed. In the bread bin, hungry ghosts.

Somewhere, elsewhere, my mother was sulking in the rain. I call up
her young face. Who did she think she was with her big words
and her belt and her beatings? Who do I think I am to write her?
She must have been sad. She must have been lonely.
Discipline. Chastisement. I stretch out my four year old hands.

Take a breath. Hold it. Let it go.

The garden again. Finglas.
My younger sister on the coalshed roof playing circus.

Early June – elderblossom, sweet pea.
The morning carries the smell of the sea.

I'm above in the boxroom looking down at her
through the window. Eldest daughter

packing what will fit in a rucksack,
what of seventeen years I can hoist on my back.

I don't know where I'm going. She steps out
on the narrow breeze block fence. If I shout

I'll startle her. She'll fall.
I swallow back a warning, the call

of her name become a lump in my throat,
something stuck there all these years, a growth

I've tried to bawl out, dance out, weep.
The inarticulate foolish gestures of grief.

She falls anyway. I could not save her.
Then or now. My younger sister

stepping out, her tongue between her teeth,
a rapt concentration that stills the world beneath her feet.

I hold my breath. A sequinned leotard,
her velvet slippers, a cast-off battered

umbrella for balance. The spotlight blinds her,
the crowd is hushed, the tiger

paces his cage, the ringmaster
idly flicks at a fly with his whip. She falters.

I hold my breath. She finds her centre.
Then or now, I could not save her.

Ectopic

The four full moons of the yellow sky
pulsate. Four full moons and I need
morphine. I need more morphine to stop the hurting.

I would gut my granny for another hit.
Someone's sewn me up and left the kitchen tap,
the Apple Mac, a rabid bat, a handy anvil

inside me. The stitches there above the mons
(Won't interfere with the bikini line ...) neat
as my own white teeth clenched and grinding in pain,

that grin up, second mouth!, at the ceiling lights, the moons! and
I will work out their complicated orbits
relative to the sun and why the stars have

all deserted me. I want to know the weight
of my little creature's soul and why its fate

has been to leave before I had a chance to save
her. Or him. It? They keep calling it *it*.
I am a woman with a sieve carrying sand

from the beach. And all this time the rain
is hammering the window pane. I count perfect feet.
Your ten perfect toes. Your perfect fingers ten. Your blue eyes, since,

perfect foetus, I must summon up the will to kill
you soon before you get too strong a grip
on the black hole that occupies the void that was my heart.

O somewhere there is a beautiful myth of sorting,
of sifting through a mountain of dross to find the one seed
whose eventual blossom is such would make a god cry.

The Bog of Moods

The first time I cross the Bog of Moods
I misread the map.
The Bog of Moons I thought it was
and watched as your white cap

lifted by a sudden squall
was cast before me unto the canal
a full moon itself on the jet black water
shattering the perfect mirror

of the starry heavens. Seeds
of light prolific as common duckweed,
fen sedge, pollution-intolerant arrowhead.
Bistort. Bulrush. Bog bean. Bur-reed.

The low down belly rooted naming
of these wet toed, turf sucking
mockers at our hamfisted, clubfooted clumsy
taking of each other. Glory be to whimsy

and misreading that have us cross the Bog
of Moots or Moos. For yes, they're there –
the slow moan of them squelching through the fog
of their own breaths, swinging full udders,

dainty hoofs picking through bladderwort
and crowfoot. Hells bells! And helleborine!
The harder you look, the more you will have seen;
and I say forgive me for the tense and curt

way I've been all day. The world
had shrunk to the proportion of the narrowboat.
I was a termagant curled
in the prickly armour of my pre-menstrual overcoat

barking at the moon, the mood,
the moot, the moos, until the moment when we stood
hand in hand under the stars and you showed me the rare
and lovely Grass of Parnassus, far

from its usual habitat. And something loosened
and came right, as if the land
herself was settling down, plumping out her skirts,
prepared to take her ease, and done with birth.

On Poetry

for Niamh Morris

Virgin

To look back then:
one particular moon snared in the willows
and there I am sleeping in my body,
a notebook beside me with girl poems in it
and many blank pages to fill
and let there be a rose and the memory of its thorn
and a scar on my thigh where the thorn had ripped

earlier that day in the abandoned garden
where he came first to me
and lifted my skirt
and we sank to the ground.

And let me be peaceful
for I wasn't.
Not then, not for many moons after.

Mother

mother you terrorist
muck mother mud mother
you chewed me up
you spat me out

mother you devourer
plucker of my soul bird
mammal self abuser
nightmatrix huntress

mother keeper
of calendar and keys
ticking off moon days
locking up the grain

mother house and tomb
your two breasts storing
strontium and lies
when you created time

mother you created plenty
you and your serpent consort
you and your nests
you and your alphabets

mother your pictographs
your mandalas your runes
your inches your seconds
your logic your grammar

mother wearing a necklace of skulls
who calls into being
by uttering the name
mater logos metric

mother your skirts
your skins your pelts
with your charms
old cow I'm your calf

mother fetishist
heart breaker
forsaker and fool
in the pouring rain

mother I stand
over your grave
and your granite headstone
and I weep

Whore

I learnt it well. I learnt it early on:
that nothing's free, that everything is priced
and easier do the business, be cute, be wized
up and sussed, commodify the fun

than barter flesh in incremental spite
the way the goodwives/girlfriends did
pretending to be meek and do as bid
while close-managing their menfolk. It wasn't right.

I believed it wasn't right. See me now –
I'm old and blind and past my sexual prime
and it's been such a long and lonely time
since I felt fire in my belly. I must allow

there'll be no chance of kindling from my trance
the spark that wakes the body into dance;
yet still comes unbidden like god's gift: an image –
a boy turns beneath me, consolatory and strange.

It Is All I Ever Wanted

for Eavan Boland

to sit by this window
the long stretched light of April falling
on my desk, to allow

the peace of this empty page
and nearing
forty years of age

to hold in these hands
that have learnt to be soothing
my native city, its hinterland

and backstreets and river scored
memory of spring
blossom and birds –

my girl-poems
fountaining
over grief and the want of someplace to call home.

Last week I took as metaphor, or at least as sign,
a strange meeting:
a young fox walking the centre line

down the south side of the Square
at three in the morning.
She looked me clear

in the eyes, both of us curious
and unafraid. She was saying –
or I needed her to say – *out of the spurious*

the real, be sure
to know the value of the song
as well as the song's true nature.

Be sure, my granny used to say,
of what you're wanting,
for fear you'd get it entirely.

Be sure, I tell myself,
you are suffering
animal like the fox, not nymph

nor sylph, nor figment,
but human heart breaking
in the silence of the street.

Familiar who grants me the freedom of the city,
my own hands spanning
the limits of pity.

Suburb

Desire Path

For days before the kids were gathering stuff –
pallets and cast-off furniture, the innards of sheds,
the guts of Barna huts. Local factories on red alert
for raiding parties under cover of dark.

I watched them lug and drag fair-got and knocked-off
gear across the park, to the gap in the hedge,
to their deep ditched hoarding spot where they kept
it dry and guarded against the rival gang's attack.

They reminded me of bees, making to the flower
or worker ants. Their comings and goings wore

the grass away until there was only bare earth
on their preferred track – a desire path

inscribed on the sward. I reckon seen from above
it must look umbilical to some object of exotic love.

Stood Up

Leaning against the tree for over an hour,
young man waiting – for his girl, I assume.
All Souls' Day and the leaves falling dreamily.
I've seen the girl he's waiting for, a flirt,

up at the pub with the shiny gang, a short time
ago. Skulling pints. She's having a baby.
At least that's the word out there on the street.
They say it's not his. The first day of winter

is sweet and mild and gold and blue. He looks
beyond the aspen's tremulous leaf
to where small children fan the embers

of last night's bonfire. They coax a flame. It sucks
the air vigorously, then hesitates, then takes like grief
that's easier borne now than it will be to remember.

Pyrolatry

'Our wheelie bin was missing after the bin collection today.
It has no. 13 painted in white on one side.
If you happen to see it, please let us know.'
Should I tell them about the flames I saw

earlier – the green and the purple and the blue. The way
they snaked and writhed, sometimes narrow, sometimes wide,
could only have been plastic, toxic and noxious, so
strong the smell on the breeze. I had to claw

the washing in, which hung for hours in Virgo
from the drying line, which reeled and jigged
through that constellation until dark fell

and the wind dropped its poisoned cargo.
The flames veered east, then north, the kids ligged
round; then someone turned up with a drum – autumn's knell.

Stink Bomb

The smell of which still hangs about the house
despite the scented candles, the essential oils
I've burned and censered through the rooms
like a priestess in a diabolic rite.

Of course the row we had could have roused
the undead and the dead alike. It left me coiled
in a foetal crouch behind the couch, some womb
I was trying to get back to. And shite

if we didn't wake next door's dog; the Hound from Hell
Himself, right on cue. You'd have to laugh. Or die
trying. Between your irrefutable logic

and my inarticulate sobs, we missed the door bell
ringing, we missed the children singing *trick
or treat, trick or treat, the ghost afloat, the witch afly.*

Mistle Thrush

The sycamore is weeping leaves of fire;
a maple stands in its own flaming lake;
shy birches isolate in yellow puddles.
You'd half expect these young trees to kick

their fallen skirts away. Bride? Bullfighter?
Dervish dancer rapt in a swirling cape?
When I went out an hour ago to muddle
through the leafdrift at my door, a flock

of mistle thrush descended – a deputation
from the wingéd world with urgent and with fatal news:
Dying is simple. You breathe in, you breathe out, you breathe in,
you breathe out and you don't breathe in again.
They acted like this was cause for celebration
– the first minor chord of my winter blues.

Sudden Rain

I'm no Buddhist: too attached to the world
of my six senses. So, in this unexpected shower,
I lift my face to its restorative tattoo,
the exultation of its anvil chime on leaf.

On my tongue I taste the bitter city furled
in each raindrop; and through the sheeted fall of grief
the glittery estate doth like a garment wear
the beauty of the morning; the sweet reek of miso

leached from composting leaves. Last night's dream
of a small man who floated in the branches of an oak
harvesting mistletoe with a golden sickle

I intuit as meaning you'll be tender and never fickle
this winter, though this may be synaesthetic
nonsense; I've little left to go on, it would seem.

Malice Aforethought

Her tongue would flense the flesh from off your back.
I've never heard her utter a good word
about a neighbour or a friend in need.
Yet half the time you'd listen to spite your self,
knowing full well tomorrow it's your turn
to squirm and be lambasted on the spit,
the faggots stacked about your feet, the match

struck and held to straw and twigs. Should it catch
and take – the whole estate is lit
in the glare and glamour, while the one who burns
discovers the heft of our black craft, our art, frail shell.
Each flaming word a falling leaf – seed
nurturer and comforter that'll one day lift a bird
from the earth to its nest, a worm in its beak.

The Tantric Master

For I shall consider his beautiful navel firstly
– an altar! – whereat I've often offered flowers,
the yellow buttercup especially, a monstrance I can elevate
to the memory of his mother who surely taught him to pet.
And honeysuckle and meadowsweet and the wild dog rose:
one for its scent, one for its sound, and one for the tone of his skin
that is all petal to me.
                        For I shall consider
secondly each individuated pore of his entire body
and consider each at length having nothing better
to do with my time, and each being a universe unto itself.
This I call rapture.
                        And thirdly, to make no bones
about it, being the crux, the hardest part of the matter,
I shall consider his noble and magical wand. He do good
business throughout the night with it. He enchant,
and spellbind and wind me round his little finger;
or, on a moony night in April, even his little toe.

Which brings me to his nails: he keepeth that trim and smooth
the better to pleasure me. So subtle his touch I can feel
the very whorls of his fingerprints and could reconstruct from
                                                        memory
his mark on my breast. Each ridge the high mountain,
each trough the deep canyon, unfathomable;
but I, having buckets of time, do fathom, do fathom.

For I shall consider the mesmeric draw of his nipples,
like standing stone circles on the broad plain of his chest,
megalithic power spots when I lay my hot cheek
on the cool of his belly and sight through the meadows
and the distant forests the trajectory of sun and other stars.

His mouth, I won't go into, being all cliché in the face of it ,
except to say the dip of his lip is most suited to suction and friction,
and other words ending in tion, tion, tion, which come to think of it
when I'm in the grip of it, is exactly how I make sweet moan.
                        For I shall consider
him whizzbang dynamo and hellbent on improving my spiritual
                                                        status.

You can keep your third eyes and your orbs sanctimonious
the opening of which my Master believes *is* the point.
He says I'm a natural and ultimate enlightenment a mere question
of time.
But in patient devotion I'll admit to deficiency. The theory of being
not a patch on just being is. Yap I distrust! Show me.
Don't tell me the way. The right place for talk of this ilk
is not during, not after, and foretalk will get you nowhere at all.
The best that I hope for in our daily instructions
is the lull between breaths, spent and near pacified.

A Woman's Right to Silence

When the silence of the grave
steals over me as it does
like a mantle that comforts each day

I fancy it could save
me, the way the fuzz
on a sweet peach, say

the one you gave
me in bed not an hour ago nuzz-
ling up and making even the grey

of this spring morning easier to bear
can save me; or those first
ash leaves that as I decide

which skirt to wear
start their slow deliberate burst-
ing from the bonny black bead,

allow me claim silence as a rare
and fine sister, not in the least a curst
state, but ecstatic, free, untried.

MARY O'MALLEY

MARY O'MALLEY

I made this selection as much as a teacher as a poet. I am thinking of myself, not as I am now, but of the young woman wrighting the poems that would become part of my first collection, and consumed by the lyrical cry of my second book, the homage to my ancestors and place, a kind of blind singing. I had left the village for the city, a warm if Catholic foreign city and had grown to love it. I had left the tribe, choosing Europe over America, Portuguese over English, living between languages in a gloriously unconscious mimicry of my child-hood. I am thinking of the young woman or man in love with the taste of words, whose intellectual rigour will learn to meet the notes of an unstoppable song rising in the throat, from whence they do not yet know or care. This is why I have included 'Credo' and 'The Spiralling Song', early imperfect prayers I will neither deny nor moderate.

'Throughout history, women have been closer to words than to silence. Talking, singing, whispering', writes Marjorie Agosin in her introduction to *These Are Not Sweet Girls*, '... though women have been close to words, they have often been barred from speaking.' In Ireland the barring order has been lifted, thanks in no small part to the work of Eavan Boland, who instilled in me early the need for intellectual as well as technical rigour.

Making this selection, I sometimes cringed at my over-intense adolescents, and I have included several here because much as I might wish at times to improve on them technically, I do not believe it would serve the purpose of this book to airbrush the imperfections, and I believe a map of the process is useful for the serious reader. Surely the poetic truth is best served by examining the spaces, the odd awkward join, the might-have-been?

I see my obsessions were set early on, that I return to the same image shop again and again, that the boats and myth-women served me well in a world where women held only a subverted authority, where in the early poems I felt a need to stake my claim in the world, as befits a woman who had no land. I was disenfranchised from my own language and shamed because of it and that has been both a rich seam mined and a chasm into which a poet might fall. So I moved slowly from my own immediate mythology towards the familiar Greeks, with their forges and boats and tribal in-fighting. I did so slowly because the right to move around among the statues is not easily earned – too often they are used as cheap decoration.

The last poem in this selection sits between fate and the next epiphany. It may be time to leave Ireland again. To hunt for the sun. These are yesterday's darlings. The lines of tomorrow's are forming between an ordinary street and the skies where destruction is gathering, almighty, steel-rich. The voices of the small people are rising. Who knows what the next breath will bring?

Credo

There is a risk
that every consideration of silk,
each velvet hush between lovers
is stolen from other women,

that consenting acts of love
are only enjoyed
over the staked thighs
of the unsaved women of El Salvador,

that I have no right
to claim kinship with war women,
their ripe bellies slit like melons
while I guard

the contentment of my children,
agonise over which small
or great talent to nurture,
which to let die.

But while I am yet free
to observe the rights of womanhood
I will relish and preserve
the sigh, the sway, the night caress

yes, and the dignity of my children.
I will anoint my wrists with scent,
fold fine sheets, hoard
sheer stockings and grow a red rose.

I will hold them all for you
in that inviolate place,
the hallowed nook beside my heart
that no man knows.

Every step I dance
each glance of love and glistening note
from a golden saxophone
is an act of love for I believe

in the resurrection of the damned.
I believe your day
is an arrow loosed,
it is burning along a silver bow

to meet you rising to your power
like a crocus in the snow.

Hormones

I wouldn't know a hormone
from a hole in the head,
if I came across one
in the street, say
or it suddenly sat up
beside me in the bed.

The only clue I have
is that they look a lot like nerves.
At least they serve much the same purpose –
the equal distribution of misery
or worse.

It would be useful
when I smash the second last sideplate
or let loose with the poker after the cat,
when I say
'It's my hormones made me do it,
they're at me again'
and he says 'What hormones?'
to have a group photograph to point to.

'There,' I'd say, 'that one with a face
like a young Beelzebub,
he made me do it,
throw the poker at poor Smoky.

You see that one with the pointy ears
and the wicked glinty little eyes,
he made me wink at the drummer
that night in the pub.'

That way too,
if I ever saw a hormone
I could take it by its scrawny little neck
and squeeze.

The Spiralling Song

If we are not shards of fire
Trapped in the hard diamonds of time

Let me sing you one pure love song
Deep from the heart. Let me swim

Back beyond the river's bend,
Beyond a bright morning in spring

When death reared; your violent red bouquet
Flung among the daffodils.

I would have plundered the margins of the monks
For haws and sloes and shining water,

And fished a flashing trout
To spread on your bare board

Instead of thinking you knew
How well you were loved, how well.

Now it is soft summer. Warm air
Has settled on the uneasy town, soothing;

I could never have shown you the nest
Where your blackbird nested, alone.

If we are not shards of fire
Trapped in the hard diamonds of time

May you inherit the high chair
And the enveloping down.

Tribute

We caravanned in the rain to Omey. The children
were let drive, mad, across the strand.
The piper stayed behind but the thread
of his wild playing held us still.
We made an odd crowd at Feichín's well
and later, clumped around a raw excavation.

As we stood there trespassing on the dead
divided between bodies and bones,
the climbers always at the edge,
I breath-heavy, could not lay my hand
on a single wild flower, only a wreath of shells.

The Shape of Saying

They call it Received English
as if it was a gift you got
by dint of primogeniture.
Maybe it was. Old gold words
toned like concert violins,
tuned to talk to God.

After the French and Latin wars
I relished the poppies of Donne
though I thought this graceful foreign tongue
was only meant for men,
alright for the likes of Coleridge
but it gave me unpleasant dreams.

They say we cannot speak it
and they are right.

It was hard and slippery as pebbles
full of cornered consonants
and pinched vowels, all said
from the front of the mouth
no softness, no sorrow, no sweet lullabies
until we took it by the neck and shook it.

We sheared it, carded it, fleeced it
and finally wove it
into something of our own,
fit for curses and blessings
for sweet talk and spite,
and the sound of hearts rending,
the sound of hearts tearing.

Cornered

As a child, were you dark or fair?
The innocent question gaffed her.

I was a dark child, and frail.
I never warmed to land

but if anyone menaced my shore
I would tooth and claw and nail

for the only thing I had,
an undiscovered continent

of swirly forests and scant
unwinding sheets of sand.

Porpoises

for Martin

Off Slyne Head at night
in a fifty-foot trawler
it is cold and black
even at midsummer.

The sky is close.
Out from the once manned rock
White electric light
Arcs over the water.

A mysterious life pulses
under the boat. Something
disturbs the even breathing
of the waves. A sound like wings

and a shape, indiscernible
in darkness, shaves the surface.
The fisherman hears
and leans over the bow.

The hairs on his neck rise
with the memory of old stories.
A school of invisible porpoises
is passing. 'Christ, they were lovely!'

Their perfect phosphorescent shapes
sculpted in the algae.

Tracing

for my father and Richard Murphy

They sit under a western window
a poet and a fisherman
tracing the geneology of pucans. Back
to the summer of nineteen-twenty-seven,
back to a rotting template in the sand.
Between them they could raise the dead.

And I forever outside looking in
am thinking of women measuring
the rising skirts of the wind, scanning
the swollen sea for one speck
to lift out of a trough,
a miracle of engine or sail

when I would rather be there
beside the black-haired men,
appeasing God with the swift sacrifice
of net to knife. What keeps me out,
the uncontented daughter?

The lines are drawn, life's soundings
etched across my face. What's underneath,
the cleansed bone, is defined below
that inner sea of age and jealousy
and rage at all the sunrises
missed in sleep. Was I betrayed by tears
or a thirst for the tender word?

I feel the heft of a satin handled
fish-knife. The poem forms,
a lobster pot turning
on a wooden wheel. The slats
are pliant and smooth. I soaked them
and peeled them bare of bark
in lessons learned under my father's eye

that things must bend to reach
a different shape. My bending
is not easy; nails are driven in.
Such work is done in winter and my hands
are pained with cold. No complaints.
He knew I wouldn't suit sewing.

Under the window I listen
to the story of a boat. They place
the keel, the boom, the tracery of ribs,
carving and caulking and laying sail.
Let me see … that would have been
nineteen-fifty-four, the year
she was born … Between them
I chart my own course and keep afloat.

Canvas Currach

I am a racer. Light, made for speed.
I hardly touch the water. Fragile
but I can carry three big men
and outlast them. It's all in the balance.
I will never drown.

I have no sail to wear but my black dress
clings to my ribs, seamless.
I am a slim greyhound of the sea.
The deeper your oars dig in
the lighter I skim.
I am built to run. Race me!

The Annunciation

History is teeming with comely maidens
awaiting godly transformations.

Leda, Yourself and the Conneely* girl
must have felt the same fear

when used as host
by swan, merman and Holy Ghost.

This given, did He have to send
such a fey announcing angel round

with a mouth like a jaded sex tourist,
or is this where God bows to the artist?

All three know the transformation
from luscious girl to Pietà

pregnant, on the run, crucified with tears
will take three months less than thirty-four years,

that you will then bear nineteen centuries
of prayers for airports, intercession, cures.

Did a trace of that plundered innocence
tint the rose windows of Notre Dame with radiance?

Here, where people carried knives
between them and marauding spirits

when they sang your lament in triplicate
in words familiar and intimate

the litany of limb and feature by destroyed mothers
stopped the hand of Gods and artists.

* The Conneelys were said, in folklore, to be descended from seals.

Song of the Wise Woman

Speak to me of tapestry
Speak to me of gold
Speak to me
Of a flowering tree
Watered by a woman's blood.

Read to me of hanging stars
Read to me of love
Read me that dark talking tree
That hides a secret child.

Sing away the dark man's touch
For I am still and cold
Sing me air and sing me fire
With your voice of Wintery gold.

Whisper me a legend
Whisper me a lie
Whisper me a flowering tree
And warm me in its fire.

Weave me in your tapestry
Thread me through with gold
But I must tend the Winter tree
Watered by a woman's blood.

The Otter Woman

Against the wisdom of shore women
she stood on the forbidden line too long
and crossed the confluence of sea and river.
One shake of her body on O'Brien's bridge
and the sea was off her.
A glorious swing from haunch to shoulder
sent water arching in the sunlight,
a fan of small diamonds flicked open,
held, fell. Her smooth pelt rose into fur.

He stood and watched her from the shadows
and moved to steal her tears
scattered on the riverbank.
Now he could take his time. He smoked.

She was all warm animal following the river,
trying her new skin like a glove.
He trailed her, magnetised by her power to transform,
the occasional bliss on her face, her awakened body.
Once or twice she saw him.
Her instincts were trusting on land.
They smiled. This took the whole Summer.

He took her by a lake in Autumn
a sliced half moon and every star out
the plough ready to bite the earth.

She left him on a street corner
with no choice and no glance back,
Spring and a bomber's moon.
In between their loosed demons
played havoc in the town.

He pinned her to the ground, his element.
This was not what she came for
but what she got.
Soon the nap of her skin rose only for him.
It was too late to turn back.
She grew heavy out of water.

Indifferent to all but the old glory
he never asked why she always walked
by the shore, what she craved,
why she never cried when every wave
crescendoed like an orchestra of bones.

She stood again on the low bridge
the night of the full moon.
One sweet deep breath and she slipped in
where the river fills the sea.
She saw him clearly in the street light – his puzzlement.
Rid of him she let out
one low strange cry for her human sacrifice,
for the death of love
for the treacherous undertow of the tribe
and dived, less marvellous forever in her element.

Couplets

She set my task and daily dutiful
I contrive black and white unbeautiful

lines. The first mistake was to read
'Midsummer' and become interested

in how the rhyming couplet
purrs and stretches for Walcott.

This is, after all, a detox programme designed
to knock the prettiness out of my lines,

toughen their hides, reduce simile
and bring the poison out in me.

The Wound

Nothing changes. The legend tells of three men
in a currach, fishing.
A big sea rose up and threatened to engulf them.

They cast lots to see who was wanted – a young man.
As the swell hung over him
he grabbed a knife and pitched in desperation,

cold steel against the wave.
The sea withdrew and all were saved.
One man heard a cry of pain and prayed.

At nightfall a woman on a white horse
enquired and found the house.
'My mistress is sick and only you can save her,'

she said and gave him guarantees.
They took the road under the sea
to a palace where a beautiful woman lay.

His knife was buried in her right breast.
'This is the knife you cast into my flesh.
You must pull it out with a single stroke

Or I will die by midnight.' He did
and the wound became a rose. She offered
the treasures of her green underworld,

a pagan kiss. The same old story. She begged:
'This scar will ache forever if you go.'
Then a choir of lost men whispered,

'Stay here and she will have your soul,'
so he blessed himself, refused and went above
to the simple solid world he understood.

Interior

'There is no domestic detail in her poems …'

There is now. Two by fours
and concrete slabs, the floors
littered with cigarette stubs.

The timber supporting the new stairs
is stalwart. 'That won't shift.'
It will of course and it's all useless

when the electrician's mate
kangoes through the live wire
playing a mean guitar.

Good golly, Miss Molly. 'Draw a straight line
up from the switch, in your mind.
That's called an image,' I told him,

but they're only interested in grouting
and gully risers, a consonance of solid things,
nuts and bolts men.

The skin of ochre paint in the bedroom
has done more to hold this house together
than a gross of six inch nails.

'There's a fault in the living room walls.
It could be the wrong shade of red – Atomic Flash.'
Like Gods, they never listen.

A Touch of Sass

Once I saw a black woman with sass
conducting English like a big band,
words danced and a jazz chant
two-stepped across the floor.
Sounds rocked and rolled, vowels
stretched and yawned and sighed
as Maya Angelou put some revolution
in the elocution class.
I closed my eyes and smiled
and thought of England.

Meditation on the Long Walk

Desire would be a simple thing
all those Gods rampant
and the earth moving for Leda;
her life transformed by his seed,
what was engendered revealed,
the mystery of what she understood
economically preserved
in a ripple of uncluttered hindsight.

Flip the coin and let the wives out.
Yeats' telling questions hang
upside down like fish-hooks
or inverted swans' necks. With her beak
savage at his loins
indifferent to all but his seed
is there talk of ecstacy and knowledge
among the tumbling feathers?

Yet there is an attractive symmetry,
that lust without responsibility
she peeled back to pure desire
him a real God, the earth
pulsing briefly like a star
and a few thousand years away
a poet trawling the night sky
for a single blinding metaphor.

The Dark House

Last night the house pulled open again.
Through the gap in the porch
big enough to let the sky in
I saw a figure on a white horse

riding across the sixpenny moon.
The beams at the gable were
six inches short of their beds
in the wall and the heavy timbered roof

strained apart slowly like a seagull
against a storm. This morning
it was whole again but I know well
they are out there lurking

until the speirbhean sends them pulling
at my shelter. She will not rob me of sleep
but what will happen to the starlings
nesting in the eaves?

These Are Not Sweet Girls*

'After every war
Someone has to tidy up.'
Wislawa Szymborska

The wounds women inflict softly on women
are worse than any lover can do
because they are more accurate. Such women
lead from behind silence. They are Ophelia's big sisters,
the marrying kind, their power mediated through men.
Their smiles hook around rivals' throats
like necklaces. They are sweet in company.

Then there are women who understand the night,
those who have read the wind correctly and know
the real business of the world
could be decided by women alone
and be better managed – but want men
for their honest lies, a door held open, a thorny rose:
they are always promising something.

I myself am happy to barter the well-run shop
for sweet rain, a hand steadying my shoulder
like a wave.
Only this morning a man's mercury shadow
ran through my fingers when I woke.
He drained through my sleep. For hours
I heard a voice in the upstairs rooms – echo, echo.

Such men are first principles – they represent themselves
poetry, lust. They lie with honesty that women lack
and take our breath away with masterpieces,
like Rodin's stolen kisses or the portraits
of Picasso's mistresses, one after another.
Somewhere between their eyes and the wine
we recognise need and admit the honest truth:

---

* *These Are Not Sweet Girls: Poetry by Latin American Women*, White Wine Press,
New York.

These are the world's great lovers,
the men who like women.
Such a man will write one hundred love poems
to wife number three
and she will let herself be taken in. Such a man
causes sensible woman to wear high heels,
skirts, hearts on our silk blouses like statues.

We pay attention briefly to our own desires
over the wants of our children
who orbit us like small moons – this is why we love them.
You Latin women are not fooled.
When he leaves you say: 'Such bastards.'
and 'Love has done this to me',
as if love happens to women

governing them like a verb, or the moon.
You laugh at his photograph appearing
in a bookshop six thousand miles away
as if that was the least he could do, you both
being Catholic. Apparitions of lovers are commonplace
In South America. Here, it's saints.
You are not nice girls.

In the face of cancer and betrayal you open the whiskey
smoke cigars and kick off your shoes.
This is the real constituency of women
where it is not enough to sweep up the mess
when unspeakable things are done
to your children. You insist
There has to be singing, a dance in the face of death.

Captain Roque

'Do you remember how we met?'
he asked me yesterday. I'm not likely to forget,
his sword at my throat. Toledo steel,
and he was damn good but a pitch of the caravelle
turned the tables. Lover, do you remember that
and the storm-tossed nights?

I'm not a woman to weaken for love
but I'd give all except the lives of my men to forgive
his attempted mutiny.
I'd say his hands pirated the garnet at my throat
the dreams from my pillow and nothing else,
but coming from a house of pirate women
I'll call him captain of his own shipwreck
and mine, like he called me his sea queen.

The Loose Alexandrines

Shameless they parade twelve by twelve by twelve across
the pages out of uniform. They wear high heels.
One with dyed blonde hair has a run in her stockings
and another of very unresolved gender

though I predict he will have a feminine end
and it serves him right – is dancing over the line
dressed in leather pants with a big star on his crotch.
It lights up – now what do you think he got that for?

Not his prosody. Look what happens as soon as
you relax the rules. First they make up their own. Soon
they're stravaiging over the pages in loose ranks
total anarchy – where's the poetry in that?

Muck savages, socialists, up from the country,
I disapprove of the regions and those people
without so much as a degree from Trinity,
with relations in Boston instead of Blackpool

marching out with the best of us. The Atlantic!
The poetic equivalent of red lipstick.
Books must be prescribed – more Larkin, less Yeats, no Plath,
no mad women – you're safe with Bishop and Clampitt.

Poetry must be strict and purge itself to survive.
It's time to round them up and herd them, twelve by twelve
by twelve into sheep pens, the lads divided from
the girls, the pigs from the pearls, the boys from the men.

Anubis in Oghery

for Oisin

Our dog, Georgie is dead. She lived
with us for ten years and walked three miles a day
with me but loved you best because she was
mostly yours. Now I have to watch your face
the reddening look, as if it might break open
and think there is something about a man's pain
that cracks like chestnuts or old timber.
It is not lubricated by tears.

You buried her down among the hazels
and blackberries, made a cairn on the grave
planted two birch trees. No one instructed you
in these rites. Yesterday you were a small boy
playing with a pup that chewed windows. Now
you walk away, a dream dog at your heel. Tall, able.

Ceres in Caherlistrane

Somewhere near forty-second street.
A girl, copper-haired, sings for a hawk-eyed man.
He tastes, in the lark's pillar of sound
honey and turf-fires. A tinker's curse rings out:

This is the voice of Ireland, of what we were.
He approves. Her hair gleams. There is a vow.
Later, she skips into the grafitti-sprayed subway.
At the edge of hearing, a laugh, a man's death cry,

A woman's love call are carried out of the tunnel's
round mouth caught in the snatch of a tune.
She has no idea these underriver walls
are shored up with Irish bones, black men's bodies.

She thinks all the buskers in New York are down
here tonight like cats. She hears them – a keen,
a skein of blues. They speed her passage. She hums,
picking up the echoes in her river-run.

In Galway, her stooked hair ripens that Summer.
At Hallowe'en there are wineapples.* A seed caught
in her teeth will keep the cleft between this world
and the next open, the all souls' chorus a filter

for certain songs that rise from a cold source.
Brandy and honey notes replace spring water –
the gift price to sing an octave deeper
than sweet, tuned to a buried watercourse.

* Wineapple is another name for the pomegranate.

In the Name of God and of the Dead Generations

I will tell you the sound the wounded make.
First let this be clear:
I always knew what belonged to me.
The piece of ground under my feet
or my sleeping body was mine
and all the land between
an imaginary line fifteen feet
above the high water mark
and the shore at low tide.
not including Manhattan
and in spring, more,

which might be why Mediterranean
coastal regions pulled me
with their small tides
or areas of high seismic activity
such as Lisbon and San Francisco –
so much for place. Yes
it has mattered, yes we replace
rock with the shimmering space
an idea of a rock where the rock has been.

Yes, I understand abstraction.
It is the welcoming place
into which strangers may come,
people with gypsy blood and skin
darker again than that
of certain fishermen along the coast
but that all said I was born outside the pale
and am outside it still. I do not fit in.

Let me tell you the sound the wounded make.
Vowels that rise out of slashed throats
will be somewhat strangled
and inelegant in our Hiberno English –
the gurgled speech of Kosovo
ringed with hard Dublin argot
from the inner city
or drawn out by tender vowels in Clare
sounds uneducated as well as broken.
This is not sexy English
not the accent to elicit
'Put a bit of butter on the spuds Andre.'

There were new Jews in Brooklyn, new Irish
in the Bronx a hundred years ago –
their 'sweedhard' and 'stoah'
unbecoming in the mouths of young men
from Carna or Warsaw. These are the sounds
the wounded make.
An old man from the Gaeltacht* at a wedding
'Excuse me, miss, I don't speak English so good'
the Miss a branding iron.
In Irish the sentence would have sung.

We have spent a small ransom
remembering the famine
that some of us never forgot
in universities all over America
and never gone looking for the ones that got away
from Mother Machree and the ancient order
of Hibernians, the black Irish.
They left in the darkened holds of coffin ships –
they arrive sealed in the holds of containers
wounded, sometimes dead, between the jigs and the reels
and the Céad Mile Faílte.**

* An area in which Irish is the first spoken language.

** An expression of welcome.

The Joiner's Bench

Somehow she found herself drawn
to his desk, that intimate place,
ran her hand over its surface
as you would smooth a skirt down.
A ridge where the lathe had skipped
delayed her and she looked up at his eyes
surprised how familiar
their blue black stain. It spread like ink.

His mind played over her poems,
her hand slipped over the scarred timber,
a wave of slim-fingered elegance. Best left at this
best to have set the ocean on fire
between them than a shared desk –
trees were her nemesis.

The Poet's Lover Names her Price

The week of the Mission in nineteen fifty-nine
a man woke up just as a cat
big as a good-sized dog, sprang.
He was black as the pit of hell
and his eyes were on fire.
A miraculous medal saved the man in the end
but the struggle was terrible.
The smell of burning coal
on flesh and fur, lingered in the room for weeks.
'The claw marks are scrawbed* on my back,' he said.

* Clawed, scratched.

He walks over the roofs
of your slip-slidy dreams.
It is not those modern demons
ineffectual in the light
you should heed –
your nights and your poems
are like suburbs. There is a price
on my love and a reward.

Do something. Perform
a pious or religious act
to attract the big cat.
Grapple the truth from him.
It will take more
than a Latin act of contrition
to break his power
but I will give you an invocation.

Let him once break your stare
and his claws will sink in
to your throat and tear.
He will discard the heart,
it's the soul he's after.
If you win, he'll disappear
leaving the smell of scorched flesh
and a poem. Worth the mess.

The Boning Hall

*'... the wreck and not the story of the wreck
the thing itself and not the myth ...'*
Adrienne Rich

No one goes diving into coffin ships but if they did
with the desire for pearls quelled they'd see wonders:
limbs streaming by, the rush of blood, oxygen, water
bubbling with the slipstream. Then the flesh stripped
to the bones, flensed and the master saying 'measure twice,
cut once, the same for a steel boat as a set of pipes.'

Bone pipes. A phosphorescent shape, not fish,
not seal-woman but essence, slips
through the eye of a needle, of a storm
past the fabulous galleons, the gold coin,
down to where the black water is
and the little open-mouthed bone-harp sings
not of the names for things you cannot say
but the long round call of the thing itself.

The Wineapple

Daughter you are moving out and it is time
for this story about Demeter and Persephone.
You'll remember most of it from when
you were small: the working mother,
a strange lustre on the leaves the child gathers,
the ground opening, the man.
He shaded his eyes from the light, not the deed –
nowadays there is nothing that cannot be told.

You are moving out into the half-way house
and this is the story of half a year, childhood robbed.
It is the mother's point of view,
and we may differ on details as night from day
as daughters and their mothers do,
except in this: flower was your first full word.
You snatched one from the maelstrom of bougainvillea
at our neighbour's gate, an offering in magenta.

Some things are fated or let us say so with hindsight
because otherwise madness lies crouched in every night.
It is never as simple as it seems, this point of view.
There are daughters emerging from the ground
and mothers entering. But back to the story, the sound
of war between a woman and the king of hell. Demeter knew
from her own begetting that the gods' weaponry was crude
and would pay any ransom. A sullen bargain was made.

The gods fight dirty. So do mothers – they claw
time back line by line. The legend is told well. It sketches
over the uglier close ups. The story is hard enough
but not uncommon. He offered marriage and girls are tough.
So Zeus said. We know the cut earth bleeds as heavily now as when
the poem was written down and before that again
when the girl paused too long – it is said she ignored warnings –
by a stream and the new fruit died on the stem.

Remember the seeds in her teeth, how she had to stay
six months of every year with her kidnapper – you won't.
But on this cusp look carefully at the two houses of your life.
Choose neither. Wine. Apple. There's enough mapped out.
Separate juice from pulp. Rent a temporary room in the sun
and try to figure out what keeps so many stars from falling.
No, hardly hope. Will it add anything to say this is neither lament
nor epithalamium? All I can give you in spite of invocation

and the calling back of hard words piercing the silence
like sub-atomic particles is a splash of holy water, good perfume.
Touching, the invisible worlds physicists believe in despite new facts
that turn their temples inside out. This is the oldest story of all.
Open-ended. Home, the point of departure and return.
Among the jumble of skirts and jumpers waiting to be packed,
the gold shoes we chose together, for the heels and thongs
are impatient to be off. These are the bookends of your song.

Prescribing the Pill

Say goodbye to the fixed idea:
a mother holding a child
looking at it in the appraising way
you would a treasured ring,
an emerald or a wedding band
with becoming pride, muted joy.

Say goodbye to that idea.
Get rid of it as if it were
a straining dog's leash
a primed shotgun.
People always say 'Let it go'
as if it were that simple
but there's recoil.

This mother has no choice.
All her life she has loved the sea, a man, hills.
Now this, the serpent coiled in her ovary.
Its black lidless eyes look out through hers
every time she makes love
and there will always be more of them.

She knows she has been blessed.
A man's lips on the underside of her wrist
his body guarding her back
led to this. She loves all her children
but this one. It is the idea's fault
and she has clutched this idea close –
see how her eyes guard it.

She's due to be churched.
The baby knows nothing of this
but all her life a hunger for cobalt blue
will course through her belly like a rip-tide.

Welsh Pastoral

i.m. R.S. Thomas

The chapels in your still valley are biblical,
the Jacob's sheep content and allegorical.

There was a honed edge in its Calvinist worship,
sad churches, empty, unused to glory.

Snow fell here. I thought of the shepherd's wives
gathered every Sunday, their cold comfort, bitten cries.

We deserve more than dead churches, envisioned pieties,
the practised ring of near-death stories.

This laudanum soaked place lured me, like a holy kiss
but we read through early imprints.

I looked back as I walked out of your painted past.
The church shifted, it rose on a tide of Aves and Kyries.

A priest, golden robed, raised the host,
drank Spanish wine. Blood flowed through the veins

of a dead congregation. The women's eyes softened,
expecting first communion. A high bell shivered.

I left the way I came in. The serious men stared
the sky moaned and every candle on the altar blazed.

The Man of Aran

But what if it were not epic.

Before the echo sounder was invented
fishermen let down weighted piano wire,
they listened for a school to hit, a note to sound.

Perhaps a scale – grace notes as single fish
hit E flat minor, say, or strange tunes
as a shoal crescendoed through the water,
minnows and sharks, sharps and flats –
heard from above at a different pitch
not perfect, but accurate, close enough for jazz;

their watery playing gave them up to slaughter
but the boatman dreamed of women singing
and the song coaxed him as he lured mackerel
with feathers that darted like blue jays
through the clear sea. He stayed out too long.

Let's leave it at that.
There would be cliffs rearing soon enough,
weather fighting.
No need for all that hauling of wrack
to the wrong side of the island,
for half drowning the locals, for shark.

We know how it works.
A pretty lure, hunger, the hook. No storm is as sweet
or deadly as the sting, the barb's sink.

Billie

Men just loved Billie.
Her unblaming pain
made them want to hurt her more
just to hear that voice soar and dip,
the little rasp, silk on a nail file, as it slid
up from her belly.

Pegeen Mike's Farewell to the Playboy

The strand is white, the tide is out,
the last ferry has pulled away from the pier.
Below a line of council houses
a red scarf lies on the sand,
a wound fading at the edges.
This is where the knife stabbed the island
again and again and again.

A breeze plays softly with skin.
A young bull roars out of memory, cut.
A timber-ended tourniquet
clips the absence off neatly.
The wind stirs the silk, fingers
the scarf, picks it up. It struts
across the limestone catwalk.

You were looking for one red image –
just a streak to relieve the grey.
You thought there were only the haws,
poison berries, a swish of fuchsia. Here, love,
adventure is not playacting. The dark man
takes his place by right.
When night falls, blades flash.

The Art of House Maintenance

He bought a house, stripped it to the bedrock, then began
rebuilding in his own image, putting himself together
over the rubble of marriages, lovers, occasional children.
He consulted her on each phase, the shape of a table – round;
the floors, pale wood; the walls, all white. She advised
colour. He refused. I lived next door. The house filled with light.

The death-light of the inland north kills shadows.
She would have known the signs with drink or dirty pictures.
By the time he unpacked the complete Carl Jung and the I Ching
she was trapped. She crouched. The house became a tabernacle
to keep her in. Emanations of white drove him to excess –
clean, he said, so clean. Spilled tea was a catastrophe.

She ran away. In Lisbon the colours are laid on thick.
Sienna and ochre powdered her skin, aboriginal dust.
The stone mosaic is satin underfoot. It was bright, hot. She dived,
swam, remembered when grey was the only colour –
cardigans, ratskin boots. Then revolution, the intimate squares
across which red carnations surged, joyous as victory or blood.

Back in her own place, she lies half drowned. I live upstairs.
On St Brigid's day she stirs. Her womb is cold.
She lights the sacred heart lamp and faces the empty rooms
without the liberated glow a therapist depends on.
Her need is naked and past its prime. Spring
he'd say, promise. Her hope rises like work to be done.

Songs from the Beehive

'For the sake of delight
Take from my hands some sun and some honey
As Persephone's bees enjoined on us.'

Osip Mandelstam

Autumn

I am not yet girl
not boy. Don't dare tell me
the kingdom of two rooms
coat covers, the river
flowing beyond the half-door
are nothing. Imprisoned fire.

Stitch this into history –
the hair on the dog
drowned under ice is the colour
of an old fox, of uaigneas,
the Irish for loneliness.

I am young still,
my belly a hole
howling to be filled. Firstborn
sole heiress to a fire in the grate,
desperate for its heat.

The hen's onyx eye pierces.
I will learn to fast her
for the kill, not fit
for the knife across her windpipe
nor to blow a shrill tune on it.

Daddy but for you
it would all be ash north of heaven.
The blue line after midnight
would flash once and grow dark.
I heard your voice last night
in a room in West Virginia.

Sisters gyre and whirl.
I try to step in on their beat
always a half-measure out.
They sweep out of reach
on the waves of a collapsing spectrum

The women of the tribe
do not fuss. They form a sealed unit.
Think how wonderful to be right
about the map of heaven
the road home.
At least sometimes.

I am old now. I can see
the sun spinning into a burning string
my fixed point going, going, gone.
The icy spikes' glow
on the holly tree
is the last brightness at the future's end.

Beyond could be anything or nothing.
It is not likely
to be the honeyplain.
While we have breath to sing,
let us or when the pain hits, scream.

Winter

Black hole, white dwarves
negative energy.
We'll arrange it all
into a neat ball of string
the end bits hidden
and unravel a skein of spectral light.

A thin girl
staring into black water
in 1975. A boy in a velvet jacket
wants to save her.
This black tide is no threat.
She steps towards it
in love with death.

Go back to her.
Let her stay as long as it takes.
No shape-shifters, no seal people
swim there – it is a sea of ink
out of which her hands will make
nothing or everything.

She knows the name
of this river and has drunk enough
to put all the ghosts under.
For years it worked.
you loved her, became the sun.
Suns expand, explode and go cold.

Walk the dry syke
the tearpath, its salt crystals
lit from within by some planetary light.
Not love, though something
holds the universe together still.

I am the girl
in the music box going round
and around in my tinkling world.
Let me wind down
or my head will explode
like a tired star. Give me your hand.

In Chicago, when you stood
by your father's grave
the wind knifed
the planes of your face raw.
A space opened around you,
frozen sound.

Wordprints. Crystal
imprints absail down the cliff
of your silence. I peered over the edge
and screamed from vertigo
and rage, beating the walls
of your chest for an echo.

This is the woman you married.
She has stood too long
looking at the Pleiades' light –
years after it has gone.
Do you know there are days when your skin
is part of mine still.

How can we count?
Twenty-two anniversaries.
Stop where? Your name is scripted
on every cell in black ink,
little rice-grains
some with Chinese characters.

The world needs re-making.
I am hopeless as a blind child.
There are unexpected ledges.
My son's arm around my shoulder
tells me where the edge is
and I step back.

Our eyes are stars,
houses. We fear eviction.
On all souls' night
a ghost horse drifts over the lake.
We wheel – we always will – between
the high and low solstices.

EAVAN BOLAND

EAVAN BOLAND

Eavan Boland was born in Dublin in 1944. Her father was a civil servant; her mother, Frances Kelly, was a noted painter. She spent five years of her childhood in Dublin and began her education at Miss Meredith's. In 1950 she went to London, attended convent school in Finchley and Hammersmith and in 1956 relocated with her family to New York.

When she returned to Dublin in 1959 she studied for the GCSE exams at the Holy Child Convent in Killiney for admission to Trinity College. Her study of Latin there was the most influential part of her education. In 1962, after leaving boarding school, she published a pamphlet called *23 Poems* and two more pamphlets of poetry in the following year.

She entered Trinity College in 1962, was awarded a First in English and graduated in 1966. Her first volume of poetry, called *New Territory*, was published in 1967. She joined the faculty of Trinity as Junior Lecturer in 1967 and resigned in 1968. She worked as a journalist for many years after that, doing freelance work and reviewing for the *Irish Times*. In 1969 she married and in 1970 moved to Dundrum, a suburb in Dublin. Her two daughters, Sarah and Eavan, were born there.

Her second book, *The War Horse*, was published with Gollancz in 1975. Her third, *In Her Own Image*, was published by Arlen House in 1980. *Night Feed* was also published by them in 1982. In 1986 she published her first volume with Carcanet, *The Journey*, which was a Poetry Book Society Choice. *Outside History* in 1990 was also a PBS choice, as was *In a Time of Violence* in 1994. In 1995 she published a prose book, *Object Lessons: The Life of the Woman and the Poet in Our Time*. *The Lost Land* was published by Carcanet in 1998 and *Code* in 2001.

W.W. Norton in the US have published *Against Love Poetry* (2001), *The Lost Land* (1998), *An Origin Like Water: Collected Poems 1967–1987* (1996), *In a Time of Violence* (1994) and *Outside History: Selected Poems 1980–1990* (1990), as well as *Object Lessons*. They are also publishers of *The Making of a Poem: A Norton Anthology of Poetic Forms* which she co-edited with Mark Strand.

In 1994 Eavan Boland was poet-in-residence at the National Maternity Hospital in Dublin and a member of its arts programme for its centenary year. With the head medical social worker, she led a group of discussion and expression for women and their partners whose babies had died in the hospital.

She has received the Lannan Award in poetry and the Literary Award of the American–Ireland Fund. In 2002 she received the Corrington Medal for Literary Excellence, the John Frederick Nims Award from Poetry Magazine and the Smartt Family prize from the Yale Review for the poems in *Against Love Poetry*, which was also a *New York Times* Notable Book of the Year. She is Director of the Creative Writing Program and the Mabury Knapp Professor in Humanities at Stanford University. She divides her time between California and Dublin, where she lives with her husband, the novelist Kevin Casey.

Athene's Song

From my father's head I sprung
Goddess of the war, created
Partisan and soldiers' physic,
My symbols boast and brazen gong,
Until I made in Athens wood
Upon my knees a new music.

When I played my pipe of bone,
Robbed and whittled from a stag,
Every bird became a lover,
Every lover to its tone
Found the truth of song and brag.
Fish sprung in the full river.

Peace became the toy of power
When other noises broke my sleep.
Like dreams I saw the hot ranks
And heroes in another flower
Than any there. I dropped my pipe
Remembering their shouts, their thanks.

Beside the water, lost and mute,
Lies my pipe and like my mind
Remains unknown, remains unknown.
And in some hollow, taking part
With my heart against my hand,
Holds its peace and holds its own.

The War Horse

This dry night, nothing unusual
About the clip, clop, casual

Iron of his shoes as he stamps death
Like a mint on the innocent coinage of earth.

I lift the window, watch the ambling feather
Of hock and fetlock, loosed from its daily tether

In the tinker camp on the Enniskerry Road,
Pass, his breath hissing, his snuffling head

Down. He is gone. No great harm is done.
Only a leaf of our laurel hedge is torn

Of distant interest like a maimed limb,
Only a rose which now will never climb

The stone of our house, expendable, a mere
Line of defence against him, a volunteer

You might say, only a crocus, its bulbous head
Blown from growth, one of the screamless dead.

But we, we are safe, our unformed fear
Of fierce commitment gone; why should we care

If a rose, a hedge, a crocus are uprooted
Like corpses, remote, crushed, mutilated?

He stumbles on like a rumour of war, huge
Threatening. Neighbours use the subterfuge

Of curtains. He stumbles down our short street
Thankfully passing us. I pause, wait,

Then to breathe relief lean on the sill
And for a second only my blood is still

With atavism. That rose he smashed frays
Ribboned across our hedge, recalling days

Of burned countryside, illicit braid:
A cause ruined before, a world betrayed.

Night Feed

This is dawn.
Believe me
This is your season, little daughter.
The moment daisies open,
The hour mercurial rainwater
Makes a mirror for sparrows.
It's time we drowned our sorrows.

I tiptoe in.
I lift you up
Wriggling
In your rosy, zipped sleeper.
Yes, this is the hour
For the early bird and me
When finder is keeper.

I crook the bottle.
How you suckle!
This is the best I can be,
Housewife
To this nursery
Where you hold on,
Dear Life.

A silt of milk.
The last suck.
And now your eyes are open,
Birth-coloured and offended.
Earth wakes.
You go back to sleep.
The feed is ended.

Worms turn.
Stars go in.
Even the moon is losing face
Poplars stilt for dawn
And we begin
The long fall from grace
I tuck you in.

Mise Éire

I won't go back to it –

my nation displaced
into old dactyls,
oaths made
by the animal tallows
of the candle –

land of the Gulf Stream,
the small farm,
the scalded memory,
the songs
that bandage up the history,
the words
that make a rhythm of the crime

where time is time past.
A palsy of regrets.
No. I won't go back.
My roots are brutal:

I am the woman –
a sloven's mix
of silk at the wrists
a sort of dove-strut
in the precincts of the garrison –

who practises
the quick frictions,
the rictus of delight
and gets cambric for it,
rice-coloured silks.

I am the woman
in the gansy-coat
on board the *Mary Belle*,
in the huddling cold,

holding her half-dead baby to her
as the wind shifts east
and north over the
water of the wharf

mingling the immigrant
guttural with the vowels
of homesickness who neither
knows or cares that

a new language
is a kind of scar
and heals after a while
into a passable imitation
of what went before.

Listen. This is the Noise of Myth

This is the story of a man and a woman
under a willow and beside a weir
near a river in a wooded clearing.
They are fugitives. Intimates of myth.

Fictions of my purpose. I suppose
I shouldn't say that yet or at least
before I break their hearts or save their lives
I ought to tell their stories and I will.

When they went first it was winter; cold,
cold through the Midlands and as far West
as they could go. They knew they had to go –
through Meath, Westmeath, Longford,

their lives unravelling like the hours of light –
and then there were lambs under the snow
and it was January, aconite and jasmine
and the hazel yellowing and puce berries on the ivy.

They could not eat where they had cooked,
nor sleep where they had eaten
nor at dawn rest where they had slept.
They shunned the densities

of trees with one trunk and of caves
with one dark and the dangerous embrace
of islands with a single landing place.
And all the time it was cold, cold:

the fields still gardened by their ice,
the trees stitched with snow overnight,
the ditches full; frost toughening lichen,
darning lace into rock crevices.

And then the woods flooded and buds
blunted from the chestnut and the foxglove
put its big leaves out and chaffinches
chinked and flirted in the branches of the ash.

And here we are where we started from –
under a willow and beside a weir
near a river in a wooded clearing.
The woman and the man have come to rest.

Look how light is coming through the ash.
The weir sluices kingfisher blues.
The woman and the willow tree lean forward, forward.
Something is near, something is about to happen;

Something more than spring
and less than history. Will we see
hungers eased after months of hiding?
Is there a touch of heat in that light?

If they stay here soon it will be summer; things
returning, sunlight fingering minnowy deeps
seedy greens, reeds, electing lights
and edges from the river. Consider

legend, self-deception, sin, the sum
of human purpose and its end; remember
how our poetry depends on distance,
aspect: gravity will bend starlight.

Forgive me if I set the truth to rights.
Bear with me if I put an end to this:
she never turned to him; she never leaned
under the sallow-willow over to him.

They never made love; not there; not here;
not anywhere; there was no winter journey;
no aconite, no birdsong and no jasmine,
no river and no woodland and no weir.

Listen. This is the noise of myth. It makes
the same sound as shadow. Can you hear it?
Daylight grays in the preceptories.
Her head begins to shine

pivoting the planets of a harsh nativity.
They were never mine. This is mine.
This sequence of evicted possibilities.
Displaced facts. Tricks of light. Reflections.

Invention. Legend. Myth. What you will.
The shifts and fluencies are infinite.
The moving parts are marvellous. Consider
how the bereavements of the definite

Are easily lifted from our heroine.
She may or she may not. She was or wasn't
by the water at his side as dark
waited above the western countryside.

O consolations of the craft.
How we put
the old poultices on the old sores,
the same mirrors to the old magic. Look.

The scene returns. The willow sees itself
drowning in the weir and the woman
gives the kiss of myth her human heat.
Reflections. Reflections. He becomes her lover.

The old romances make no bones about it.
The long and short of it. The end and the beginning.
The glories and the ornaments are muted.
And when the story ends the song is over.

The Emigrant Irish

Like oil lamps we put them out the back,

of our houses, of our minds. We had lights
better then, newer than, and then

a time came, this time and now
we need them. Their dread makeshift example.

They would have thrived on our necessities.
What they survived we could not even live.
By their lights now it is time to
imagine how they stood there, what they stood with,
that their possessions may become our power.

Cardboard. Iron. Their hardships parcelled in them.
Patience. Fortitude. Long-suffering
in the bruise-colored dusk of the New World.
And all the old songs. And nothing to lose.

The Journey

for Elizabeth Ryle

*'Immediately cries were heard. These were the loud wailing of infant
souls weeping at the very entrance-way; never had they had their
share of life's sweetness for the dark day had stolen them from their
mothers' breasts and plunged them to a death before their time.'*
Virgil, The Aeneid, Book VI

And then the dark fell and 'there has never'
I said 'been a poem to an antibiotic:
never a word to compare with the odes on
the flower of the raw sloe for fever

'or the devious Africa-seeking tern
or the protein treasures of the sea-bed.
Depend on it, somewhere a poet is wasting
his sweet uncluttered metres on the obvious

'emblem instead of the real thing.
Instead of sulpha we shall have hyssop dipped
in the wild blood of the unblemished lamb,
so every day the language gets less

'for the task and we are less with the language.'
I finished speaking and the anger faded
and dark fell and the book beside me
lay open at the page Aphrodite

comforts Sappho in her love's duress.
The poplars shifted their music in the garden,
a child startled in a dream,
my room was a mess –

the usual hardcovers, half-finished cups,
clothes piled up on an old chair –
and I was listening out but in my head was
a loosening and sweetening heaviness,

not sleep, but nearly sleep, not dreaming really
but as ready to believe and still
unfevered, calm and unsurprised
when she came and stood beside me

and I would have known her anywhere
and I would have gone with her anywhere
and she came wordlessly
and without a word I went with her

down down down without so much as
ever touching down but always, always
with a sense of mulch beneath us,
the way of stairs winding down to a river

and as we went on the light went on
failing and I looked sideways to be certain
it was she – misshapen, musical Sappho –
the scholiast's nightingale

and down we went, again down
until we came to a sudden rest
beside a river in what seemed to be
an oppressive suburb of the dawn.

My eyes got slowly used to the bad light.
At first I saw shadows, only shadows.
Then I could make out women and children
and, in the way they were, the grace of love.

'Cholera, typhus, croup, diptheria'
she said, 'in those days they racketed
in every backstreet and alley of old Europe.
Behold the children of the plague'.

Then to my horror I could see to each
nipple some had clipped a limpet shape –
suckling darknesses – while others had their arms
weighed down, making terrible pietàs

She took my sleeve and said to me, 'be careful.
Do not define these women by their work:
not as washerwomen trussed in dust and sweating,
muscling water into linen by the river's edge

'nor as court ladies brailled in silk
on wool and woven with an ivory unicorn
and hung, nor as laundresses tossing cotton,
brisking daylight with lavender and gossip.

'But these are women who went out like you
when dusk became a dark sweet with leaves,
recovering the day, stooping, picking up
teddy bears and rag dolls and tricycles and buckets –

'love's archaeology – and they too like you
stood boot deep in flowers once in summer
or saw winter come in with a single magpie
in a caul of haws, a solo harlequin'.

I stood fixed. I could not reach or speak to them.
Between us was the melancholy river,
the dream water, the narcotic crossing
and they had passed over it, its cold persuasions.

I whispered, 'let me be
let me at least be their witness,' but she said
'what you have seen is beyond speech,
beyond song, only not beyond love;

'remember it, you will remember it'
and I heard her say but she was fading fast
as we emerged under the stars of heaven,
'there are not many of us; you are dear

'and stand beside me as my own daughter.
I have brought you here so you will know forever
the silences in which are our beginnings,
in which we have an origin like water,'

and the wind shifted and the window clasp
opened, banged and I woke up to find
the poetry books stacked higgledy piggledy,
my skirt spread out where I had laid it –

nothing was changed; nothing was more clear
but it was wet and the year was late.
The rain was grief in arrears; my children
slept the last dark out safely and I wept.

The Black Lace Fan My Mother Gave Me

It was the first gift he ever gave her,
buying it for five francs in the *Galeries*
in pre-war Paris. It was stifling.
A starless drought made the nights stormy.

They stayed in the city for the summer.
They met in cafes. She was always early.
He was late. That evening he was later.
They wrapped the fan. He looked at his watch.

She looked down the Boulevard des Capucines.
She ordered more coffee. She stood up.
The streets were emptying. The heat was killing.
She thought the distance smelled of rain and lightning.

These are wild roses, appliqued on silk by hand,
darkly picked, stitched boldly, quickly.
The rest is tortoiseshell and has the reticent,
clear patience of its element. It is

a worn-out, underwater bullion and it keeps,
even now, an inference of its violation.
The lace is overcast as if the weather
it opened for and offset had entered it.

The past is an empty cafe terrace.
An airless dusk before thunder. A man running.
And no way now to know what happened then –
none at all – unless, of course, you improvise:

The blackbird on this first sultry morning,
in summer, finding buds, worms, fruit,
feels the heat. Suddenly she puts out her wing –
the whole flirtatious span of it.

The Achill Woman

She came up the hill carrying water.
She wore a half-buttoned, wool cardigan.
A tea-towel round her waist.

She pushed the hair out of her eyes with
her free hand. And put the bucket down.

The zinc-music of the handle on the rim
tuned the evening. An Easter moon rose.
In the next door field a stream was
a fluid sunset. And then stars.

I remember the cold rosiness of her hands.
She bent down and blew on them like broth.
And round her waist, on a white background,
in coarse, woven letters, the words *glass cloth*.

And she was nearly finished for the day.
And I was all talk, raw from College.
Week-ending at a friend's cottage
with one suitcase and the set text
of the court poets of the Silver Age.

She stayed putting down time until
the evening turned cold without warning.
She said goodnight and started down the hill.

The grass changed from lavender to black.
The trees turned back to cold outlines.
You could taste frost.

But nothing now can change the way I went
indoors, chilled by the wind,
and made a fire
and took down my book
and opened it
and failed to comprehend

the harmonies of servitude,
the grace music gives to flattery
and language borrows from ambition

and how I fell asleep oblivious to
the planets clouding over in the skies,
the slow decline of the spring moon.
The songs crying out their ironies.

That the Science of Cartography is Limited

– and not simply by the fact that this shading of
forest cannot show the fragrance of balsam,
the gloom of cypresses
is what I wish to prove.

When you and I were first in love we drove
to the borders of Connacht
and entered a wood there.

Look down you said: this was once a famine road.

I looked down at ivy and the scutch grass
rough-cast stone had
disappeared into as you told me
in the second winter of their ordeal, in

1847, when the crop had failed twice,
Relief Committees gave
the starving Irish such roads to build.

Where they died, there the road ended

and ends still and when I take down
the map of this island, it is never so
I can say here is
the masterful, the apt rendering of

the spherical as flat, nor
an ingenious design which persuades a curve
into a plane,
but to tell myself again that

the line which says woodland and cries hunger
and gives out among sweet pine and cypress,
and finds no horizon

will not be there.

Lava Cameo

(A brooch carved on volcanic rock)

I like this story —

My grandfather was a sea-captain.
My grandmother always met him when his ship docked.
She feared the women at the ports —

except that it is not a story,
more a rumour or a folk memory,
something thrown out once in a random conversation;
a hint merely.

If I say wool and lace for her skirt and
crepe for her blouse
in the neck of which is pinned a cameo,
carved out of black, volcanic rock;

if I make her pace the cork docks, stopping
to take down her parasol as a gust catches
the silk tassels of it —

then consider this:

there is a way of making free with the past,
a pastiche of what is
real and what is
not, which can only be
justified if you think of it

not as sculpture but syntax:

a structure extrinsic to meaning which uncovers
the inner secret of it.

She will die at thirty-one in a fever ward.
He will drown nine years later in the Bay of Biscay.
They will never even be
sepia, and so I put down

the gangplank now between the ship and the ground.
In the story, late afternoon has become evening.
They kiss once, their hands touch briefly.
Please,

look at me, I want to say to her: show me
the obduracy of an art which can
arrest a profile in the flux of hell.

Inscribe catastrophe.

Love

Dark falls on this mid-western town
where we once lived when myths collided.
Dusk has hidden the bridge in the river
which slides and deepens
to become the water
the hero crossed on his way to hell.

Not far from here is our old apartment.
We had a kitchen and an Amish table.
We had a view. And we discovered there
love had the feather and muscle of wings
and had come to live with us,
a brother of fire and air.

We had two infant children one of whom,
was touched by death in this town
and spared: and when the hero
was hailed by his comrades in hell
their mouths opened and their voices failed and
there is no knowing what they would have asked
about a life they had shared and lost.

I am your wife.
It was years ago.
Our child is healed. We love each other still.
Across our day-to-day and ordinary distances
we speak plainly. We hear each other clearly.

And yet I want to return to you
on the bridge of the Iowa river as you were,
with snow on the shoulders of your coat
and a car passing with its headlights on:

I see you as a hero in a text –
the image blazing and the edges gilded –
and I long to cry out the epic question
my dear companion:

Will we ever live so intensely again?
Will love come to us again and be
so formidable at rest it offered us ascension
even to look at him?

But the words are shadows and you cannot hear me.
You walk away and I cannot follow.

The Pomegranate

The only legend I have ever loved is
The story of a daughter lost in hell.
And found and rescued there.
Love and blackmail are the gist of it.
Ceres and Persephone the names.
And the best thing about the legend is
I can enter it anywhere. And have.
As a child in exile in
A city of fogs and strange consonants,
I read it first and at first I was
An exiled child in the crackling dusk of
The underworld, the stars blighted. Later
I walked out in a summer twilight
Searching for my daughter at bed-time.
When she came running I was ready
To make any bargain to keep her.
I carried her back past whitebeams.
And wasps and honey-scented buddleias.
But I was Ceres then and I knew

Winter was in store for every leaf
On every tree on that road.
Was inescapable for each one we passed.
And for me. It is winter
And the stars are hidden.
I climb the stairs and stand where I can see
My child asleep beside her teen magazines,
Her can of Coke, her plate of uncut fruit.
The pomegranate! How did I forget it?
She could have come home and been safe
And ended the story and all
Our heart-broken searching but she reached
Out a hand and plucked a pomegranate.
She put out her hand and pulled down
The French sound for apple and
The noise of stone and the proof
That even in the place of death,
At the heart of legend, in the midst
Of rocks full of unshed tears
Ready to be diamonds by the time
The story was told, a child can be
Hungry. I could warn her. There is still a chance.
The rain is cold. The road is flint-coloured.
The suburb has cars and cable television.
The veiled stars are above ground.
It is another world. But what else
Can a mother give her daughter but such
Beautiful rifts in time?
If I defer the grief I will diminish the gift.
The legend will be hers as well as mine.
She will enter it. As I have.
She will wake up. She will hold
The papery, flushed skin in her hand.
And to her lips. I will say nothing.

Anna Liffey

Life, the story goes,
Was the daughter of Cannan,
And came to the plains of Kildare.
She loved the flat-lands and the ditches
And the unreachable horizon.
She asked that it be named for her.
The river took its name from the land.
The land took its name from the woman.

A woman in the doorway of a house.
A river in the city of her birth.

There, in the hills above my house,
The river Liffey rises, is a source.
It rises in rush and ling heather and
Black peat and bracken and strengthens
To claim the city it narrated.
Swans. Steep falls. Small towns.
The smudged air and bridges of Dublin.

Dusk is coming.
Rain is moving east from the hills.

If I could see myself
I would see
A woman in a doorway
Wearing the colours that go with red hair.
Although my hair is no longer red.

I praise
The gifts of the river.
Its shiftless and glittering
Re-telling of a city,

Its clarity as it flows,
In the company of runt flowers and herons,
Around a bend at Islandbridge
And under thirteen bridges to the sea.
Its patience at twilight –
Swans nesting by it,
Neon wincing into it.

Maker of
Places, remembrances,
Narrate such fragments for me:

One body. One spirit
One place. One name.
The city where I was born.
The river that runs through it.
The nation which eludes me.

Fractions of a life
It has taken me a lifetime
To claim.

I came here in a cold winter.

I had no children. No country.
I do not know the name for my own life.

My country took hold of me.
My children were born.

I walked out in a summer dusk
To call them in.

One name. Then the other one.
The beautiful vowels sounding out home.

Make of a nation what you will
Make of the past
What you can –

There is now.
A woman in a doorway.

It has taken me
All my strength to do this.

Becoming a figure in a poem.

Usurping a name and a theme.

A river is not a woman.
    Although the names it finds,
        The history it makes
And suffers –
    The Viking blades beside it,
        The muskets of the Redcoats,
            The flames of the Four Courts
Blazing into it
    Are a sign.
        Any more than
A woman is a river,
    Although the course it takes,
        Through swans courting and distraught willows,
Its patience
    Which is also its powerlessness,
        From Callary to Islandbridge,
            And from source to mouth,
Is another one.
                And in my late forties
Past believing
    Love will heal
        What language fails to know
And needs to say –
    What the body means –
        I take this sign
And I make this mark:
    A woman in the doorway of her house.

A river in the city of her birth.
The truth of a suffered life.
The mouth of it.

The seabirds come in from the coast
The city wisdom is they bring rain.
I watch them from my doorway.
I see them as arguments of origin —
Leaving a harsh force on the horizon
Only to find it
Slanting and falling elsewhere.

Which water —
The one they leave or the one they pronounce —
Remembers the other?

I am sure
The body of an aging woman
Is a memory
And to find a language for it
Is as hard
As weeping and requiring
These birds to cry out as if they could
Recognise their element
Remembered and diminished in
A single tear.

An aging woman finds no shelter in language.
She finds instead
Single words she once loved
Such as 'summer' and 'yellow'
And 'sexual' and 'ready'
Have suddenly become dwellings
For someone else —
Rooms and a roof under which someone else
Is welcome, not her. Tell me,
Anna Liffey,
Spirit of water,
Spirit of place,

How it is on this
Rainy autumn night
As the Irish sea takes
The names you made, the names
You bestowed, and gives you back
Only wordlessness?

Autumn rain is
Scattering and dripping
From car-ports
And clipped hedges.
The gutters are full.

When I came here
I had neither
Children nor country.
The trees were arms.
The hills were dreams.

I was free
To imagine a spirit
In the blues and greens,
The hills and fogs
Of a small city.

My children were born.
My country took hold of me.
A vision in a brick house.
Is it only love
That makes a place?

I feel it change.
My children are
Growing up, getting older.
My country holds on
To its own pain.

I turn off
The harsh yellow
Porch light and
Stand in the hall.
Where is home now?

Follow the rain
Out to the Dublin hills.
Let it become the river.
Let the sprit of place be
A lost soul again.

In the end
It will not matter
That I was a woman. I am sure of it.
The body is a source. Nothing more.
There is a time for it. There is a certainty
About the way it seeks its own dissolution.
Consider rivers.
They are always en route to
Their own nothingness. From the first moment
They are going home. And so
When language cannot do it for us,
Cannot make us know love will not diminish us,
There are these phases of the ocean
To console us.
Particular and unafraid of their completion.
In the end
Everything that burdened and distinguished me
Will be lost in this:
I was a voice.

The Dolls' Museum in Dublin

The wounds are terrible. The paint is old.
The cracks along the lips and on the cheeks
cannot be fixed. The cotton lawn is soiled.
The arms are ivory dissolved to wax.

Recall the Quadrille. Hum the waltz.
Promenade on the yacht-club terraces.
Put back the lamps in their copper holders.
The carriage wheels on the cobbled quays.

And recreate Easter in Dublin.
Booted officers. Their mistresses.
Sunlight criss-crossing College Green.
Steam hissing from the flanks of horses.

Here they are. Cradled and cleaned,
Held close in the arms of their owners.
Their cold hands clasped by warm hands,
Their faces memorised like perfect manners.

The altars are mannerly with linen.
The lilies are whiter than surplices.
The candles are burning and warning:
Rejoice, they whisper. After sacrifice.

Horse-chestnuts hold up their candles.
The Green is vivid with parasols.
Sunlight is pastel and windless.
The bar of the Shelbourne is full.

Laughter and gossip on the terraces.
Rumour and alarm at the barracks.
The Empire is summoning its officers.
The carriages are turning: they are turning back.

Past children walking with governesses,
Looking down, cossetting their dolls,
then looking up as the carriage passes,
the shadow chilling them. Twilight falls.

It is twilight in the dolls' museum. Shadows
remain on the parchment-coloured waists,
are bruises on the stitched cotton clothes,
are hidden in the dimples on the wrists.

The eyes are wide. They cannot address
the helplessness which has lingered in
the airless peace of each glass case:
To have survived. To have been stronger than

a moment. To be the hostages ignorance
takes from time and ornament from destiny. Both.
To be the present of the past. To infer the difference
with a terrible stare. But not feel it. And not know it.

The Blossom

A May morning.
Light starting in the sky.

I have come here
after a long night,
its senses of loss,
its unrelenting memories of happiness.

The blossom on the apple tree is still in shadow,
its petals half-white and filled with water at the core,
in which the freshness and secrecy of dawn are stored
even in the dark.

How much longer
will I see girlhood in my daughter?

In other seasons
I knew every leaf on this tree.
Now I stand here
almost without seeing them

and so lost in grief
I hardly notice what is happening
as the light increases and the blossom speaks,
and turns to me with blonde hair and my eyebrows
and says –

imagine if I stayed here,
even for the sake of your love
what would happen to the summer?
To the fruit?

Then holds out a dawn-soaked hand to me
whose fingers I counted at birth
years ago.

And touches mine for the last time.

And falls to earth.

Formal Feeling

A winged god
came to a woman at night.

Eros you know the story. You ordained it.

The one condition was she did not see him.

So it was dark when he visited her bed.
And it was good. She felt how good it was.
But she was curious. And lit a lamp.
And saw his nakedness. And he fled.

Into the dark. Into the here and now
and air and quiet of an Irish night
where I am writing at a darkening window
about a winged god and his lover,

watching the lines and stanzas and measures,
which were devised for these purposes,
disappearing as the shadows close
in around the page
under my hand.

How can I know a form unless I see it?
How can I see it now?

I propose
the light she raised over his sleeping body
angered heaven because it made clear
neither his maleness nor his birth, nor
his face dreaming, but

the place where the sinew of his wings
touched the heat of his skin
and flight was brought down –

To this. To us. To earth.

Eros look down.
See as a god sees
what a myth says: how a woman still
addresses the work of man in the dark of the night:

The power of a form. The plain
evidence that strength descended here once.
And mortal pain. And even sexual glory.

And see the difference.
This time – and this you did not ordain –
I am changing the story.

Mother Ireland

At first
   I was land.
      I lay on my back to be fields
and when I turned
      on my side
         I was a hill
under freezing stars.
      I did not see.
         I was seen.
Night and day
      words fell on me.
            Seeds. Raindrops.
Chips of frost.
   From one of them
      I learned my name.
            I rose up. I remembered it.
Now I could tell my story.
   It was different
      from the story told about me.
And now also
   it was spring.
      I could see the wound I had left
in the land by leaving it.
      I travelled west.
            Once there
   I looked with so much love
      at every field
    as it unfolded
      its rusted wheel and its pram chassis
          and at the gorse-
bright distances
   I had been
      that they misunderstood me.
     Come back to us
they said.
     Trust me I whispered.

The Necessity for Irony

On Sundays,
when the rain held off,
after lunch or later,
I would go with my twelve year old
daughter into town,
and put down the time
at junk sales, antique fairs.

There I would
lean over tables,
absorbed by
lace, wooden frames,
glass. My daughter stood
at the other end of the room,
her flame-coloured hair
obvious whenever –
which was not often –

I turned around.
I turned around.
She was gone.
Grown. No longer ready
to come with me, whenever
a dry Sunday
held out its promises
of small histories. Endings.

When I was young
I studied styles: their use
and origin. Which age
was known for which
ornament: and was always drawn
to a lyric speech, a civil tone.
But never thought
I would have the need,
as I do now, for a darker one:

Spirit of irony,
my caustic author
of the past, of memory, –
and of its pain, which returns
hurts, stings – reproach me now,
remind me
that I was in those rooms,
with my child,
with my back turned to her,
searching – oh irony! –
for beautiful things.

Thankëd be Fortune

Did we live a double life?
        I would have said
                we never envied
the epic glory of the star-crossed.
        I would have said
                we learned by heart
the code marriage makes of passion –
                duty dailyness routine.
But after dark when we went to bed
under the bitter fire
                of constellations,
        orderly, uninterested and cold –
                at least in our case –
in the bookshelves just above our heads,
        all through the hours of darkness,
                men and women
wept, cursed, kept and broke faith
        and killed themselves for love.
                Then it was dawn again:
Restored to ourselves,
        we woke early and lay together
listening to our child crying, as if to birdsong,
        with ice on the windowsills
                and the grass eking out
        the last crooked hour of starlight.

How We Made a New Art on Old Ground

A famous battle happened in this valley.
                              You never understood the nature poem.
Till now. Till this moment – if these statements
                    seem separate, unrelated, follow this

silence to its edge and you will hear
                    the history of air: the crispness of a fern
or the upward cut and turn around of
                    a fieldfare or thrush written on it.

The other history is silent: the estuary
                    is over there. The issue was decided here:
Two kings prepared to give no quarter.
                    Then one king and one dead tradition.

Now the humid dusk, the old wounds
                    wait for language, for a different truth:
When you see the silk of the willow
                    and the wider edge of the river turn

and grow dark and then darker, then
                    you will know that the nature poem
is not the action nor its end: it is
                    this rust on the gate beside the trees, on

the cattle grid underneath our feet,
                    on the steering wheel shaft: it is
an aftermath, an overlay and even in
                    its own modest way, an art of peace:

I try the word *distance* and it fills with
                    sycamores, a summer's worth of pollen
And as I write *valley* straw, metal
                    blood, oaths, armour are unwritten.

Silence spreads slowly from these words
                    to those ilex trees half in, half out
of shadows falling on the shallow ford
                    of the south bank beside Yellow island

as twilight shows how this sweet corrosion
                        begins to be complete: what we see
is what the poem says:
                        evening coming – cattle, cattle-shadows –

and whin bushes and a change of weather
                        about to change them all: what we see is how
the place and the torment of the place are
                        for this moment free of one another.

Quarantine

In the worst hour of the worst season
        of the worst year of a whole people
a man set out from the workhouse with his wife.
He was walking – they were both walking – north.

She was sick with famine fever and could not keep up.
        He lifted her and put her on his back.
He walked like that west and west and north.
Until at nightfall under freezing stars they arrived.

In the morning they were both found dead.
        Of cold. Of hunger. Of the toxins of a whole history.
But her feet were held against his breastbone.
The last heat of his flesh was his last gift to her.

Let no love poem ever come to this threshold.
        There is no place here for the inexact
praise of the easy graces and sensuality of the body.
There is only time for this merciless inventory:

Their death together in the winter of 1847.
        Also what they suffered. How they lived.
And what there is between a man and woman.
And in which darkness it can best be proved.

Irish Poetry

for Michael Hartnett

We always knew there was no Orpheus in Ireland.
No music stored at the doors of hell.
No god to make it.
No wild beasts to weep and lie down to it.

But I remember an evening when the sky
was underworld-dark at four,
when ice had seized every part of the city
and we sat talking –
the air making a wreath for our cups of tea.

And you began to speak of our own gods.
Our heartbroken pantheon.

No Attic light for them and no Herodotus
But thin rain and dogfish and the stopgap
of the sharp cliffs
they spent their winters on.

And the pitch-black Atlantic night:
how the sound
of a bird's wing in a lost language sounded.

You made the noise for me.
Made it again.
Until I could see the flight of it: suddenly

the silvery lithe rivers of the south-west
lay down in silence
and the savage acres no one could predict
were all at ease, soothed and quiet and

listening to you, as I was. As if to music, as if to peace.

SELECT BIBLIOGRAPHY

Paula Meehan

Poetry

Return and No Blame, Beaver Row Press, Dublin, 1984.
Reading the Sky, Beaver Row Press, Dublin, 1986.
The Man Who Was Marked by Winter, The Gallery Press, Oldcastle, 1991.
Reprinted 1992, 1994, and 1999. North American edition with
foreword by Eavan Boland, EWU Press, Spokane, 1994.
Pillow Talk, The Gallery Press, Oldcastle, 1994. Reprinted 1997, 2000.
Mysteries of the Home: A Selection of Poems, Bloodaxe Books, Newcastle
upon Tyne, 1996.
Dharmakaya, Carcanet Press, Manchester, 2000. Reprinted 2000.
North American edition, Wake Forest University Press, Winston-
Salem, 2001.

Plays

Kirkle (for children 4 to 7 years), produced Dublin 1995, Team Theatre
Company.
The Voyage (for children 9 to 12 years), produced Dublin 1997, Team
Theatre Company.
Mrs Sweeney, produced Dublin 1997, Rough Magic Company.
Published New Island Books, Dublin, 1999.
Cell, produced Dublin 1999, Calypso Company. Published New
Island Books, Dublin, 2000.
Janey Mac is Going to Die, radio play, broadcast RTE Radio 1, 2001,
repeated 2002.

Mary O'Malley

Poetry

A Consideration of Silk, Salmon Publishing, Galway, 1990.
Where the Rocks Float, Salmon Publishing, Galway, 1993.

The Knife in the Wave, Salmon Publishing, Galway, 1997.
Asylum Road, Salmon Publishing, Galway, 2001.
The Boning Hall, Carcanet Press, Manchester, 2002.

Eavan Boland

Poetry

New Territory, Allen Figgis Press, Dublin, 1967.
The War Horse, Gollancz, London, 1975.
In Her Own Image, Arlen House, Dublin, 1980.
Introducing Eavan Boland, Ontario Review Press, Princeton, 1981.
Night Feed, Arlen House, Dublin and Carcanet Press, Manchester, 1982.
The Journey, Arlen House, Dublin and Carcanet Press, Manchester, 1986.
Outside History: Selected Poems 1980–1990, Carcanet Press, Manchester and W.W. Norton, New York, 1990.
In a Time of Violence, Carcanet Press, Manchester and W.W. Norton, New York, 1994.
An Origin Like Water: Collected Poems, 1967–1987, W.W. Norton, New York, 1996.
Collected Poems, Carcanet Press, Manchester, 1996.
The Lost Land, Carcanet Press, Manchester and W.W. Norton, New York, 1998.
Against Love Poetry, W.W. Norton, New York, 2001.
Code, Carcanet Press, Manchester and and W.W. Norton, New York, 2001.

Prose and Editions

A Kind of Scar: The Woman Poet in a National Tradition, Attic Press, Dublin, 1989.
Object Lessons: The Life of the Woman and the Poet in our Time, Carcanet Press, Manchester and W.W. Norton, New York, 1995.
The Making of a Poem: A Norton Anthology of Poetic Forms, co-edited with Mark Strand, W.W. Norton, New York, 2000.

INDEX OF FIRST LINES

INDEX OF TITLES